High Scorer's Choice Series

IELTS 5 Practice Tests

General Set 1

(Tests No. 1-5)

High Scorer's Choice Series, Book 2
IELTS 5 Practice Tests, General Set 1 (Tests No. 1–5)
ISBN 9780987300935
Copyright © 2017 Simone Braverman, Robert Nicholson.
First Edition April 2017
Updated February 2023

Available in print and digital formats
Accompanying audio recordings to be downloaded on the following webpage:
https://www.ielts-blog.com/ielts-practice-tests-downloads/

To contact the authors:
Email: simone@ielts-blog.com
Website: www.ielts-blog.com

Acknowledgements

The authors hereby acknowledge the following websites for their contributions to this book (see the webpage below for a complete list):

www.ielts-blog.com/acknowledgements/

While every effort has been made to contact copyright holders it has not been possible to identify all sources of the material used. The authors and publisher would in such instances welcome information from copyright holders to rectify any errors or omissions.

Praise for
High Scorer's Choice Practice Tests

"I am a teacher from Australia. I had a Chinese friend who is studying for the exam and I used these [tests] to help him. I think the papers are very professional and useful. Many of the commercial practice papers are not culturally sensitive but this was not a problem with your tests."
- *Margaretta from Australia*

"I found out that your practice papers are excellent. I took my IELTS on March 11th and got an Overall Band 8 with listening – 8, reading – 9, writing – 7 and speaking – 7. I spent one month on preparation."
- *Dr Yadana from London, UK*

"I must tell you that the sample tests I have purchased from you have been the key to my preparation for the IELTS. Being employed full time I do not have the time to attend classes. I downloaded the material and made myself practice a few hours every 2 or 3 days for 3 weeks and was successful on my first trial. I was able to get an average of 7.5 and I was aiming at 7."
- *Oswaldo from Venezuela*

High Scorer's Choice IELTS Books

Academic   General

Academic		General
Tests 1-5	Set 1	Set 1 Tests 1-5
Tests 6-10	Set 2	Set 2 Tests 6-10
Tests 11-15	Set 3	Set 3 Tests 11-15
Tests 16-20	Set 4	Set 4 Tests 16-20
Tests 21-25	Set 5	Set 5 Tests 21-25
Tests 26-30	Set 6	Set 6 Tests 26-30

CONTENTS

Download Audio Content

In order to download the audio content please use a desktop computer (not a mobile device) with a reliable internet connection and open the following webpage in your browser:

https://www.ielts-blog.com/ielts-practice-tests-downloads/

Follow instructions on the webpage to save all audio files on your computer. The files are in mp3 format and you will need an audio player to listen to them (any modern computer has that type of software preinstalled).

Need help with audio content? Contact the author via email simone@ielts-blog.com and expect a quick response.

How to prepare for IELTS

There are two ways for you to use these practice tests for your exam preparation. You can either use them to work on your technique and strategy for each IELTS skill, or you can use them to simulate a real exam and make sure you will do well under time pressure.

Option 1   Use practice tests to work on your IELTS skills (no time limits)

To prepare well for the IELTS exam you need to have a strategy for each sub-test (Listening, Reading, Writing and Speaking). This means knowing what actions to take, and in which order, when you receive a test paper. If you are working with the IELTS self-study book "Ace the IELTS – How to Maximize Your Score", all the necessary tips are located in the book. You need to read and then apply these tips and techniques when you are practicing on some of these tests. Don't time yourself, concentrate on learning the techniques and making sure they work for you.

If you purchased the practice tests in digital format, you will need to print out some pages, for easier learning and to be able to work in the same way as in the real test (on paper). Print the Listening questions and the Reading passages and questions. You can read the Writing and Speaking questions from your computer or mobile device, to save paper and ink. If you have the paperback format, this doesn't apply to you. Use Table of Contents on the previous page to navigate this book.

If Listening is one of your weaker skills, use audio transcripts while listening to recordings, when you hear words or sentences that you don't understand. Stop the recording, rewind, locate in the transcript the sentence you had a problem with, read it, and then listen to the recording again. In the audio transcripts the sentences with answers are underlined for easy learning.

If Reading is hard for you, after doing the Reading test use the Reading Answer Help section of these practice tests to understand why the answers in the Answer key are correct. It will show you the exact locations of the answers in the Reading passages.

To compare your own writing to high-scoring samples go to Example Writing Answers and read them. Note the way the information is grouped and the tone (formal/informal) used in Writing Task 1, and the way an essay is organised in Writing Task 2.

To practice in Speaking, either read to yourself the Speaking test questions or get a friend to help with that. Record your answers and then listen to the recording. Note where you make long pauses while searching for the right word, pay attention to your errors and your pronunciation. Compare your own performance to that of students in sample interviews, and read their Examiner's reports.

Option 2   Use practice tests to simulate the real test (strict time limits)

This option will require some prep work before you can start a simulated test. Print out or photocopy the blank Test Answer Sheets for Listening and Reading and prepare some ruled paper on which to write your Writing Task 1 and 2. Also, think of a way to record yourself in the Speaking sub-test. Get a watch, preferably with a timer. Allocate 3 hours of uninterrupted time.

1. Be in a quiet room, put the Listening questions in front of you and start playing the recording. Answer questions as you listen, and write your answers next to the questions in the book.

2. When the recording has finished playing, allocate 10 minutes to transfer all your Listening answers to the Listening Answer Sheet. While you are transferring the answers check for spelling or grammatical errors and if you missed an answer, write your best guess.

3. Put the Reading passages and questions in front of you and set the timer to 60 minutes. Begin reading passages and answering questions. You can write the answers next to the questions or straight on the Answer Sheet. Remember that you don't get extra time to copy answers to the Answer Sheet, and that when 60 minutes are up all your answers must be written on the Answer Sheet.

4. Put the Writing questions in front of you and set the timer to 60 minutes. Make sure you don't use more than 20 minutes for Task 1, including proofreading time, and that you don't use more than 40 minutes for Task 2, with proofreading included.

5. Put the Speaking questions in front of you and begin the interview (remember to record your answers). In Part 2 take the whole 1 minute to prepare your speech and make notes, and then try to speak for 2 minutes (set the timer before you start talking).

6. When you have finished the whole test, take some time to rest, as you may be tired and it may be hard for you to concentrate. Then check your answers in the Listening and Reading against the correct ones in the Answer key, compare your writing tasks to the Example Writing tasks and your recorded speaking to the example interview. Analyse and learn from any mistakes you may find, and especially notice any problems with time management you may have encountered.

   Remember, it is OK to make mistakes while practicing as long as you are learning from them and improving with every test you take.

   Good luck with your exam preparation!

PRACTICE TEST 1

LISTENING

 Download audio recordings for the test here: https://www.ielts-blog.com/ielts-practice-tests-downloads/ Need help with audio content? Contact the author via email simone@ielts-blog.com and expect a quick response.

PART 1   Questions 1 – 10

Questions 1 – 5

Complete Angela's lost property form below.

Write **NO MORE THAN TWO WORDS AND/OR A NUMBER** from the listening for each answer.

**Central Cinemas
Lost Property Form**

For the attention of:	Mr. Smith (responsible for lost property)
Customer's Name:	Peter (**1**) _____
Address:	(**2**) _____ Winchester Road Alton
Postcode:	W12 (**3**) _____
Telephone:	Mobile: 01743 062 496
Film Watched:	*Spiderman*
Film Start Time:	(**4**) _____ p.m.
Seat (if known):	(**5**) _____

Questions 6 – 10

Choose **FIVE** letters, **A - L.**

What **FIVE** items does Peter's wallet contain?

A   Some business cards

B   Some money

C   A debit card

D   A note of PIN numbers for cards

E   Company identification

F   Company photocopy card

G   A cinema ticket

H   A theatre ticket

I   A hotel card key

J   A library card

K   A health insurance card

L   A passport

PART 2   *Questions 11 - 20*

Questions 11 – 15

*Below is a plan of the conference reception room with **11** locations marked (**A - K**). Questions **11 - 15** list 5 locations in and next to the conference reception room. Match the locations in questions **11 - 15** with the correct locations on the map and write the correct letter (**A - K**) next to questions **11 - 15**.*

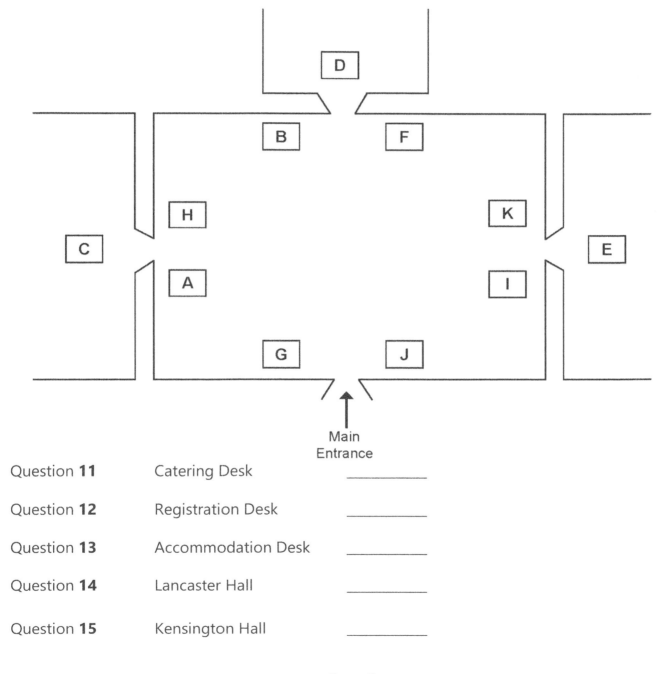

Question **11**   Catering Desk   _____

Question **12**   Registration Desk   _____

Question **13**   Accommodation Desk   _____

Question **14**   Lancaster Hall   _____

Question **15**   Kensington Hall   _____

Questions 16 – 20

Answer the questions below. Write **NO MORE THAN THREE WORDS AND/OR A NUMBER** from the listening for each answer.

16   What food will be available on the tables in the mornings before the first speeches?

17   On what floor is the conference centre's restaurant?

18   How many choices of main course will there be at lunch for vegans?

19   Where will tea be served if the weather is good?

20   Where will Linda be found at lunch times?

PART 3   Questions 21 – 30

Questions 21 – 25

Complete the notes below. Write **NO MORE THAN THREE WORDS AND/OR A NUMBER** from the listening for each answer.

Coastal Erosion Course

Locations

Australia: Almost 36,000 km of coast with approx. (**21**) _____ made of sand. A lot of the course is focused here.

California: The Pacific threatens (**22**) _____ on the coastline here.

West Africa: Human factors - such as sand and gravel removal, and construction of ports, harbours and jetties (with dredging).

Natural factors - waves, tide, sea currents + winds ((**23**) _____ could affect these as well).

Others: UK, Louisiana and Hawaii.

Field Trips

Only in Australia. The main trip is to the Gold Coast and various (**24**) _____ there. Some trips are (**25**) _____. Lots of work and fun!

Questions 26 – 30

Complete the table below.

Write **NO MORE THAN TWO WORDS** from the listening for each answer.

Type of Assessment	Number	Focus	Weighting
Essays	6	Different areas of the course. Causes, (**26**) _____ and reactions.	35%
Project	1	Students' choice - most choose an Australia topic. Mostly (**27**) _____ choose an overseas topic.	50%
Exam	1	(**28**) _____ long. Good knowledge of whole course expected.	15%
* Only the (**29**) _____ can be re-done. Students are carefully selected and the (**30**) _____ try and spot students under-performing and help them.			

PART 4   *Questions 31 – 40*

Questions 31 and 32

Complete the table below.

*Write **NO MORE THAN TWO WORDS** from the listening for each answer.*

Penguins

Description	Flightless, but excellent swimmers. Body, feet, tail and flippers all aid swimming. Feathers are waterproof with woolly down and a deposit of (**31**)_____ underneath to keep them warm.
Food	Small fish + krill.
Predators	Leopard seals + (**32**) _____ in the sea; skuas and sheathbills on land.
Classification	Debated - 17 - 20 species of penguins. 4 species live on and around the Antarctic continent; the others in sub-Antarctic regions.

Questions 33 – 35

*Choose the correct letter **A**, **B**, or **C**.*

33   The breeding sites for emperor penguins

   A   must be close to the sea.
   B   must be close to feeding grounds.
   C   must be on stable ice.

34   The egg of the emperor penguin

   A   is protected during incubation by the father.
   B   is protected during incubation by the mother.
   C   is protected on the feet of both the mother and the father.

35   The reason for the decline in numbers of emperor penguins at Pointe Géologie is

   A   due to the loss of ice there.
   B   unknown.
   C   due to warmer temperatures.

Questions 36 – 40

Complete the summary below on the threats to emperor penguins.

Write **NO MORE THAN TWO WORDS AND/OR A NUMBER** from the listening for each answer.

Threats to Emperor Penguins

The leopard seal is the principal predator of the emperor penguin, but birds can also eat eggs and young chicks, and (**36**) _____ reduces the emperor penguin's food source.

A less than (**37**) _____ Celsius upward change in temperature can cause changes in the Antarctic ice and could hinder 40 per cent of emperor penguins' attempts to find suitable (**38**) _____. The changes could cause a 20 per cent reduction in emperor penguin numbers.

Too much ice - greater distances to and from the sea to get food for the young and male.

Too little ice - (**39**) _____ can break up.

It's hoped that emperor penguins may adapt.

King penguins could displace emperor penguins, as they have a longer breeding season and survive better with less accessibility to (**40**) _____.

READING

SECTION 1   *Questions 1 – 14*

Questions 1 – 7

*There are 6 advertisements **A – F** on the next page.*

*Answer the questions below by writing the letters of the appropriate advertisements in boxes **1 – 7** on your answer sheet.*

1   Which advertisement says people can buy a used computer?

2   Which advertisement says that there are special offers available?

3   Which advertisement offers training on computer programming?

4   Which advertisement offers an opportunity to learn about history?

5   Which advertisement offers a service to improve Internet speed?

6   Which advertisement has a service to install a computer?

7   Which advertisement says that further details are available online?

A   KENTON COMPUTERS
KENTON'S BIGGEST STOCKIST OF COMPUTERS AND ACCESSORIES

Kenton Computers is the area's most prestigious outlet for buying a new computer. We sell all types of desktop and laptop computers for individual and company requirements. We also offer a complete set-up service to ensure that your purchase is used to its optimum potential.

We are also the area's specialist for gamers. Whether you're just starting out or have been gaming for years, we'll have a gaming PC and game selection to suit your level and budget.

Sale on now - 25% off all sales of new computers

B Kenton Computer Repair Service

Come to us for all your computer repair needs

- 20 years' experience; no fix, no fee
- Repairs
- Upgrades and updates
- Servicing
- 2nd hand sales
- Virus removal
- Desktops, laptops, PC's, Macs

38 Railway Road, Kenton
Tel 08462 859 823

C   Magna Computer Training Services

Here at Magna, we have 15 years of experience teaching people how to use computers. This can range from teaching people to use a computer for the first time to programming courses that can lead to a professional qualification and a job. Check our online brochure for details of all our courses and fees.

www.magnatraining.com

D   Situation Vacant

Well-known high street insurance company requires a top performing computer programmer and technician to oversee upgrades to various branches around the country. Travel conditions, pay and other benefits will be outstanding for the right candidate. Experience and references are essential. Call David Johnson on 07770 692132 for details.

E   Internet Supermarket

Want to get online or get a better connection?

Is your home Wi-Fi up to the job?

We'll show you how to beat slow connections with a new AC router and how your home's plug sockets can boost your signal with our *Powerage* technology.

We can offer you contracts with all the largest Internet providers. Drop in and tell us your requirements and we will fix you up with the best contract for your situation.

49 Longford Street, Kenton
Tel 08462 589472

F   Kenton Museum
Special Free Exhibition
The History of the Computer

From the use of the ancient abacus to Lovelace and Babbage's 19th century work to code breaking in World War 2 to the development of the Internet. Come and learn how today's essential science, household and business tool was developed.

Questions 8 – 14

Do the following statements agree with the information given in the text?

*In boxes **8 – 14** on your answer sheet write:*

TRUE	*if the statement agrees with the information*
FALSE	*if the statement contradicts the information*
NOT GIVEN	*if there is no information on this*

8   It takes three days to complete the Beginner Diving Course at the Atlantis Dive Centre.

9   Reduced fees for diving courses are possible if a large group books together.

10   Beginner divers must produce proof of identity when enrolling in a course.

11   Early stage pregnancy will not affect acceptance on a diving course.

12   The Atlantis Dive Centre only teaches diving to beginners.

13   Children between 16 and 18 can do the course if accompanied by a parent.

14   The Atlantis Dive Centre can arrange accommodation with a local family.

Atlantis Dive Centre
Become a Scuba Diver!

Take our Beginner Diver Certificate in our fully equipped dive centre, located next to the warm waters of the Pacific Ocean. The Beginner Diver Certificate takes place over three days and comprises theory tuition, confined training dives in our own swimming pool at our centre and four open water dives in the Ocean with an instructor. Once you have passed your Beginner Diver Certificate, you can dive independently at any dive centre around the world. The Beginner Diver Certificate costs AUS$600. This fee must be paid before the start of the course.

We only run the Beginner Diver Certificate with a minimum of five learner divers, but we can offer the course with three divers on payment of a supplement of AUS$300 per learner diver. For parties of six or more, we can offer attractive discounts.

It is not essential to be extremely fit in order to scuba dive, but participants on our course should possess a fundamental level of good health. In many places it is compulsory to undergo a medical test before the course begins and this is a requirement with us and all learner divers must complete a recreational diver medical. This can be done at our centre and is included within the Beginner Diver Certificate fee. If your medical is done elsewhere, you MUST bring your certificate of diving health BEFORE you begin. The following medical issues might affect your eligibility to take our diving course:
- Are you pregnant, or are you trying to get pregnant?
- Do you take any prescription medications?
- Are you over 45 years of age and smoke, have high cholesterol or blood pressure, have a family history of heart attack or stroke, or have diabetes?

Course participants must also be able to swim and this will be tested in our Open Water Swimming Test.

Although we specialise in training new scuba divers, we run monthly advanced courses that cater for more experienced divers who wish to learn new skills and gain more advanced diving certification.

One great way to learn diving is to use the new referral system. We can teach you all the theory and give you your confined water dives at our centre, and then you can choose to do your four open water dives at any recognised diving centre anywhere in the world. You tell us where you want to go and we'll send your chosen centre all the required paperwork.

For those participants coming from further afield, we can also arrange accommodation for you. We are in contact with a variety of local hotels, guesthouses, bed and breakfasts, and even campsites or homestay households. These have all been carefully vetted and we ensure that previous participants give us feedback on their experiences. We are therefore confident that we can provide the best accommodation options for you while you are doing your diving course. The regular business that we provide our accommodation partners also allows us to secure discounts for our customers, making our choices even more advantageous for you.

*For further information, consult our webpage, email us or call us directly on **000**. We will be happy to provide you with more information and we make every effort to tailor a product to your requirements.*

SECTION 2   *Questions 15 – 27*

Questions 15 – 21

Complete the summary below.

*Write **NO MORE THAN TWO WORDS** from the text for each answer.*

*Write your answers in boxes **15 - 21** on your answer sheet.*

Basic Advice for an Interview

Being late for an interview shows bad planning, bad (**15**) _____, a lack of respect, and it gives a bad first impression. Plan your journey - use the Internet and make some notes. Try to be 10 - 15 mins early, but don't come too early!

Come early *AND* come smart. Dressing informally also might give employers a poor impression of you, so make an effort with how you look.

An interview should be a (**16**) _____, so prepare lots of questions on the company and its (**17**) _____. Do more than just research the interviewing company's website. Know what the different (**18**) _____ of the company are and how you'll be a part of them.

Whatever your reasons for wanting a new job are, don't criticise your previous employer - you don't want to be seen as a (**19**) _____.

Because getting a good job is a very (**20**) _____ process, it's important to (**21**) _____ and show you're passionate about the job and the company.

Basic Advice for an Interview

1   Don't Be Late

I know this advice may sound trivial and something that you already know, but it still happens. You can never predict what might make you late. It could be just public transport problems, but most of the time arriving late is because you didn't plan properly. Running late not only suggests poor time management, but also shows a lack of respect for the company. Arriving late is an excellent way to give your interviewer a bad first impression and we all know how important first impressions are. Plan your journey as well as possible, even by checking the public transport website the night before if you have to. Jump on the Internet and figure out exactly where your interview is and make note of a couple of reference points so that you don't get flustered if you get lost. Budget your time so that you make it to the interview at least ten to fifteen minutes early. While it's good to arrive early, don't get there 3 hours early or you'll come across as nervous and well, a bit weird.

2   Dress Smartly

Some people feel that dressing down shows their character, but many employers feel that not dressing formally for an interview also shows a lack of respect and care. There's nothing to lose by putting on a tailored skirt with smart jacket or a trouser suit for a woman, or a suit for a man, so just do it and don't take a chance.

3   Ask Questions

A lot of candidates tend to think that an interview is the process of being asked questions. This is far from the truth, as both interviewer and interviewee ought to create a dialogue. You should be ready with your own questions too. A good interviewer will usually allow for enough time to let you ask as many questions as you want at the end of the discussion. Therefore, prepare questions on the topics you're interested in. Ask questions about the company and show that you want to know about their products. You don't want to show a complete lack of knowledge of what the company does; you want to show an interest. Hiring managers will assume that you have investigated their organisation's website, so expand the scope of your research efforts. Try to understand what the organisation's goals are in the short, medium and long term and how your work will contribute.

4   Don't Bad-Mouth Previous Employers

Some people apply for a new job because they're searching for a new challenge, or because they want a higher salary, and others because their employer sucks. Regardless of what your reason is (but in particular if it's the latter), don't ever say bad things about your current or previous employers in an interview. The interviewer will be listening to your answers and thinking about what it would be like to work with you. You may come across as a complainer and the interviewer may even wonder what will happen once you'll leave their company.

5   Be Enthusiastic

The job market is highly competitive and for every good position, there are usually a large number of candidates. If you've done well enough to make it to the interview, don't give the impression that you're bored with the interview, or the company. Smile and show you're enjoying everything. Employers want to hire people who are passionate about their job and interested in their company.

Questions 22 – 27

Do the following statements agree with the views of the writer of the text?

In boxes 22 - 27 on your answer sheet write:

YES	*if the statement agrees with the writer's views*
NO	*if the statement doesn't agree with the writer's views*
NOT GIVEN	*if it is impossible to say what the writer thinks about this*

22   As they're outside normal working hours, overtime rates can fall below rates for the minimum wage.

23   Employers have the right to stop any worker from doing overtime, regardless of contractual details.

24   Workers cannot work part-time in government industries.

25   Any overtime payment will be at least what is paid for a half hour's work at the overtime scales agreed.

26   Workers who have signed up for overtime must cancel their agreement in writing if they change their minds.

27   Food must be provided for workers on meal breaks on night shifts.

Working Overtime - Official Advice for Employees

Employers don't have to pay workers for overtime. However, employees' average pay for the total hours worked mustn't fall below the National Minimum Wage. An employee's employment contract should usually include details of any overtime pay rates and how they're worked out.

Employees only have to work overtime if their contract says so. If it's not in the contract, an employee can agree to work longer, but this agreement must be in writing and signed by the employee. Unless an employee's contract guarantees them overtime, their employer can stop them from working it. However, their employer can't discriminate against anyone, e.g. by stopping some employees from working overtime while letting others do so.

Overtime must also be reasonable. Overtime can be reasonable so long as the following things are taken into account:
- any risk to health and safety from working the extra hours
- the employee's personal situation, including their family responsibilities
- the needs of the workplace
- if the employee is entitled to receive overtime payments or penalty rates for working the extra hours
- if they are paid at a higher rate on the understanding that they work some overtime
- if the employee was given enough notice that they may have to work overtime
- if the employee has already stated they can't ever work overtime
- the usual patterns of work in the industry.

Unless it says differently in a part-time worker's employment contract, their employer will usually only pay overtime if they work:
- longer hours than set out in the employment contract
- more than the normal working hours of full-time staff and full-time staff would get extra pay for working these hours
- unsocial hours (e.g. late at night), for which full-time staff would get more pay

Employees who work overtime have to be paid a minimum of thirty minutes of work at overtime rates. For example, if an employee works fifteen minutes overtime, they will need to be paid for thirty minutes.

Normally, most workers do not have to work on average more than forty-eight hours per week unless they agree. Even if they do agree, they have the right to opt out at any time by giving written notice. The average working week is calculated by taking the average over a seventeen week reference period. Workers who wish to opt out must give notice in writing of at least seven days. A longer period of notice may be agreed by the employer, but it can be no longer than three months.

An employee who works more than four hours of overtime on a Saturday morning has to get a ten-minute paid break. An employee who works for five hours or more on any day must get at least one meal break.

Young people (sixteen and seventeen year olds) cannot work more than forty hours per week and they cannot opt out.

SECTION 3   *Questions 28 – 40*

Read the following passage and answer Questions 28 – 40.

The History and Production of Lipstick

Most people know that lipstick has been around for quite a while, but it is less well known that it has been in use for more than four thousand years. Lip and facial paints go back even further, being used for various purposes and not only by women, but also men. Hunters applied facial and lip paint as means of camouflage. Priests and religion-related officials used it to worship their gods and honour their beliefs, and lots of people have used it to enhance their appearance to attract the opposite sex, which is still common today. Cosmetics, specifically lipstick, have captivated mankind since prehistoric times, mostly due to their ability to support people's individuality, improve their appearance and hence boost their confidence.

It is difficult to determine exactly who invented lipstick, but it is believed that the plant and fruit juices applied by men and women of ancient civilizations were the predecessors of the lipstick we know today. Not only favoured due to their appearance-enhancing properties, these juices have also always been used for medicinal purposes. Because lip tissue lacks the pigment melanin, responsible for skin colour and the protection from ultraviolet rays, lipstick can protect the sensitive skin of lips from dry winds, moisture and sun. From 2000 BC to 100 AD, ancient Mesopotamia and Egypt were the centres for cosmetics to develop, amongst others lipsticks and lip balms. It was at this time that carmine became a main constituent of lipstick. This pigment is made from crushed insects and is still used today. Only wealthy women, such as the legendary pharaoh, Cleopatra, had access to these expensive cosmetics.

During the European Middle Ages, lipstick experienced its lowest point in terms of popularity. Wars, poor living and health conditions, as well as little to no advancements in the arts and sciences eliminated lipstick from the minds of many people, who focused primarily on the procurement of food and other survival essentials. Although cosmetics in France still retained popularity during the Middle Ages with the moneyed classes, it was only during the nineteenth century that they truly became publicly popular and accessible again. It was then that, due to industrial and technological advancements, French cosmetologists began the production of lipstick for commercial sales, which allowed the popularity of lipstick to reappear. New inventions, such as innovative colours, shine formulas as well as flavoured lipstick became the trends and adapted to the ever-changing fashion moods, which still rule the development of new lipsticks today.

Nowadays, common ingredients of lipstick include wax and oil, which simplify the application process, alcohol, which is used as a solvent to dissolve these ingredients, and finally, pigment, which ensures a wide variety of shades and colours. Some brands even incorporate lead, which can be harmful when ingested. Furthermore, preservatives, antioxidants and fragrance can be added, which is done in order to ensure a longer shelf life. This can also be done by storing it in the fridge. This prolongs the life of the lipstick in terms of delaying the degrading process of its ingredients.

Lipstick ingredients have been under the spotlight recently, as discoveries by a US consumer group have found traces of the above-mentioned lead in several lipsticks exceeding regulations by the Food and Drug Administration (FDA). In tests, FDA scientists developed an analytical method for measuring the amount of lead in lipstick. Their findings confirmed that the amount of lead found in lipstick is very low and does not pose safety concerns. This did lead though to ingredient lists being required on lipstick packaging, much like is found on food. However, the popularity of lipstick has not suffered. Organic lipstick is now available and lipstick remains in widespread use, which it will presumably continue to do over the next centuries.

The manufacturing of lipstick has unarguably changed over the last four thousand years, but the basic formula has remained the same, both in terms of ingredients and methods of production. When creating a new lipstick, chemists need to consider the contemporary fashion mood. This also affects how the lipstick is presented to the public and its appearance is contingent on the requirements of the cosmetics brands.

A carefully monitored procedure is essential in order to enhance the quality and effect of the final lipstick product. Generally, the manufacturing process can be summarised in six stages. In the first stage, the chosen pigment or a combination of pigments is mixed with various types of oils. A three-roll mill then grinds every particle until its size is minimised to at least twenty microns, one micron being one thousandth of a millimetre. In the second stage, the pigment mixture is merged with wax, which is accomplished in a kettle surrounded by steam and powered by a propelled agitator. Then, in order to get rid of 'cold-marks', which are unwanted products of fast cooling, the heated lipstick liquid at around eighty degrees Celsius is poured into vertical split moulds. These usually have temperatures of around thirty-five degrees Celsius. Finally, the lipstick is cooled down, taken out of the moulds and is prepared for flaming, a process that involves exposing the lipstick to an open flame. This ensures the better appearance of the lipstick and enhances its ability to protect itself from external influences such as air, moisture or heat. The product is then ready for packaging and labelling.

Questions 28 – 33

*Complete each sentence with the correct ending (**A - K**) below.*

*Write the correct letter (**A - K**) in answer boxes **28 - 33** on your answer sheet.*

28   Hunters of prehistoric times applied colour to

29   The human race has been fascinated by lipstick's ability to

30   Lipstick's medicinal usefulness includes its advantage to

31   Mesopotamia and Egypt were the first areas to

32   Due to manufacturing progress, make-up producers in France were able to

33   Recent findings by an American customer organisation caused new official directives to

A   ensure that the ingredients dissolve well.

B   enhance personal uniqueness and attractiveness.

C   lead to more success at work.

D   include carmine as one of lipstick's ingredients.

E   shield the body from harmful external factors, such as natural elements.

F   create a shiny surface on lipstick.

G   melt the lipstick's ingredients completely.

H   eliminate carmine as one of lipstick's ingredients.

I   ensure that they were well concealed in their surrounding environment.

J   draw the public's attention towards lipstick and what is in it.

K   reintroduce lipstick's widespread use through producing it on a larger scale.

Questions 34 – 36

Answer the questions below.

Write **NO MORE THAN THREE WORDS** from the text for each answer.

Write your answers in boxes **34 - 36** on your answer sheet.

34   In which country in the Middle Ages were cosmetics still commonly used by the rich?

35   Where should you keep your lipstick if you want it to last for longer?

36   On whom does the distinct packaging and labelling of lipsticks depend?

Questions 37 – 40

Label the diagram below. Write **NO MORE THAN THREE WORDS** from the text for each answer.

Write your answers in boxes **37 - 40** on your answer sheet.

The Lipstick Manufacturing Process

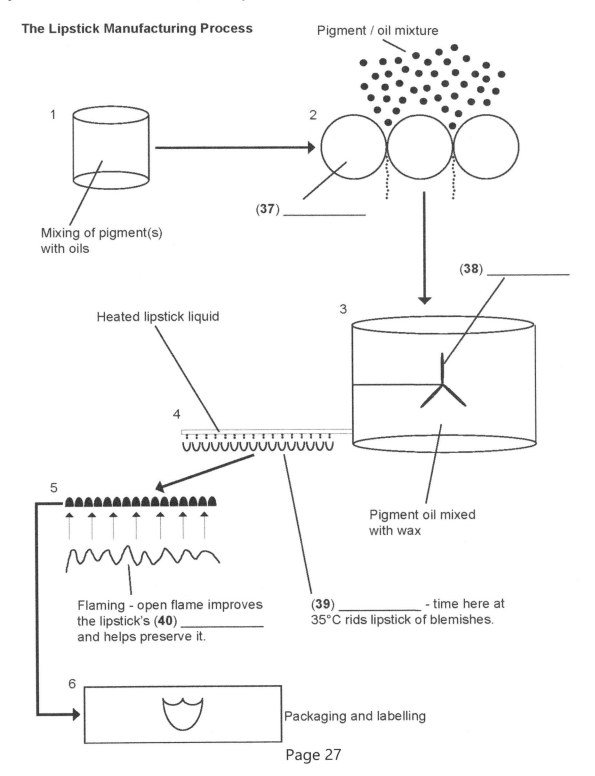

Pigment / oil mixture

1

2

(37) _____

Mixing of pigment(s)
with oils

(38) _____

Heated lipstick liquid

3

4

5

Pigment oil mixed
with wax

Flaming - open flame improves
the lipstick's (40) _____
and helps preserve it.

(39) _____ - time here at
35°C rids lipstick of blemishes.

6

Packaging and labelling

WRITING

WRITING TASK 1

You should spend about 20 minutes on this task.

> **You recently noticed a local restaurant that was offering a part-time job.**
>
> **Write a letter to the restaurant's manager. In your letter,**
>
> - **explain that you would like to apply for the job**
> - **give some details of any relevant experience that you have**
> - **specify the days and times that would suit you**

You should write at least 150 words.

*You do **NOT** need to write any addresses. Begin your letter as follows:*

> ***Dear Sir / Madam,***

WRITING TASK 2

You should spend about 40 minutes on this task.

Write about the following topic:

> **Recently published figures show that the wildlife population around the world has decreased by around fifty per cent over the last fifty years.**
>
> **What can we do to help protect the wildlife round the world?**

Give reasons for your answer and include any relevant examples from your knowledge or experience.

You should write at least 250 words.

SPEAKING

PART 1

- Can you tell me a little about where you live?
- Which is your favourite room in the house/flat where you live?
- What changes would you like to make to where you live?

Topic 1   Fruits and Vegetables
- Do you like fruits and vegetables? What fruits and vegetables are popular in your country?
- Why are fruits and vegetables so good for people?
- How can we get young people to eat more fruits and vegetables?
- Do you think you could ever be a vegetarian? (Why/Why not?)

Topic 2   The Weather
- What are the typical seasonal weather conditions in your country?
- How do you think weather can affect people's moods?
- Do you feel weather patterns are changing nowadays? (Why?)
- What do people like to do in your country when it's raining?

PART 2

Describe your ideal car. You should say:
    what kind of car you'd like
    what special features you'd like it to have
    where you'd like to travel in it
and explain why it would be your ideal car

PART 3

Topic 1   The Advantages and Disadvantages of Cars
- What are some of the advantages and disadvantages of owning a car?
- Do you think cars should be banned from city centres? (Why/Why not?)
- What other measures can governments introduce to stop people using cars so much?
- How do you feel that cars will be improved over the next 50 years?

Topic 2   Driving and the Law
- At what age should be people be allowed to start driving and what age should they stop? (Why?)
- What are the laws like regarding driving speeds in your country?
- What laws does your country have about driving and alcohol?
- Do you feel there should be a law about how long one can drive without stopping?

PRACTICE TEST 2

LISTENING

Download audio recordings for the test here:
https://www.ielts-blog.com/ielts-practice-tests-downloads/
Need help with audio content? Contact the author via email
simone@ielts-blog.com and expect a quick response.

PART 1   *Questions 1 – 10*

Questions 1 – 5

Answer the questions below. Write **NO MORE THAN THREE WORDS AND/OR A NUMBER** *from the listening for each answer.*

1   In what month is Katherine's birthday?

2   What is Katherine's last name?

3   At what time would Katherine like the party to start?

4   What activity is not available on the chosen date?

5   How many people will Katherine invite to the party?

Questions 6 – 10

Complete the information sheet and price list for John's outdoor center below.

Write **NO MORE THAN TWO WORDS AND/OR A NUMBER** *from the listening for each answer.*

John's Outdoor Centre

Opening Times:　　　Monday – Friday　　　7 a.m. – 8 p.m.
　　　　　　　　　　Saturday & Sunday　8:30 a.m. - **(6)** _____p.m.

<u>Price List</u>

Activities	Bonfire	$15
	Boat Tour	$**(7)** _____ per person
	Cycling Tour	$8 per person
	Hiking Tour	$25 per person
	Baking (15 people max)	$**(8)** _____ per person
Food & Drinks	Small Buffet	$200
	Large Buffet	$**(9)** _____
	Lamb on a Spit	$35
Staying Overnight	Camping with Tents	$40 per tent (4 people per tent)
	Tipi	$80 per tipi (20 people per tipi)
	Tree House	$**(10)** _____ (20 people)

PART 2   *Questions 11 - 20*

Questions 11 – 14

*Below there is a map of the town of Barton with the locations of features of interest (**A - T**) of Sharon's walking tour marked on it. Match the locations in questions **11 - 14** with the correct locations on the map and write the correct letter (**A - T**) next to questions **11 - 14**.*

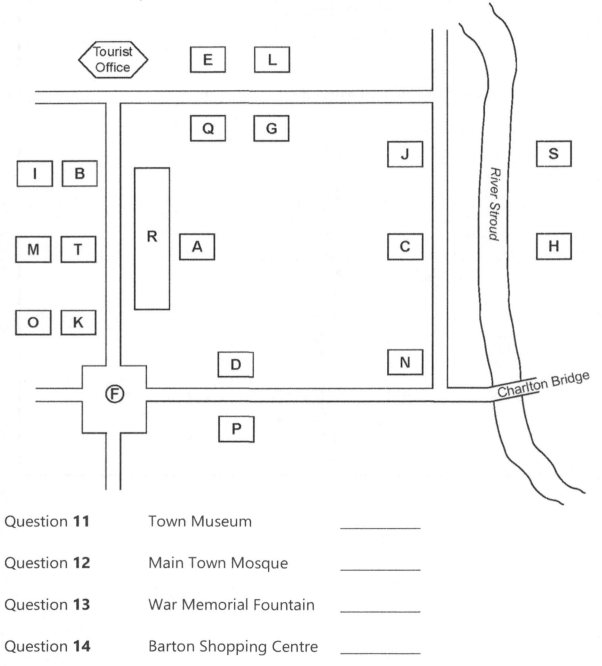

Question **11**	Town Museum	_____
Question **12**	Main Town Mosque	_____
Question **13**	War Memorial Fountain	_____
Question **14**	Barton Shopping Centre	_____

Questions 15 and 16

*Choose the correct letter **A**, **B**, or **C**.*

15   For how long does Sharon estimate her walking tour of the town will last?

     A   2½ hours

     B   2 hours + 20 minutes

     C   3 hours

16   How much does Sharon charge for her walking tour of the town?

     A   20 pounds

     B   5 pounds

     C   Nothing

Questions 17 – 20

*Choose **FOUR** letters, **A** - **H**.*

What **FOUR** things does Sharon say people can do that evening in Barton?

A   Watching live music

B   Watching live football

C   Watching films

D   Going on a tour of the town's theatre

E   Watching a play at the town's theatre

F   Taking part in a quiz

G   Watching some theatre performed in the town square

H   Watching tennis on television

PART 3   Questions 21 – 30

Questions 21 – 25

Complete the table below.

Write **NO MORE THAN ONE WORD** from the listening for each answer.

Students' Agriculture Project Progress		
Student	Project	Notes
Steve	How parasites affect the growth rates of potatoes.	* Steve interacted with (**21**) _____ to gather his data. * Steve had to rent a (**22**) _____ himself to gather data on growth with parasites. * Steve sold his potatoes and made a profit.
Simone	A study of the speed of (**23**) _____ for different tomato varieties.	* Simone used a university greenhouse to use for growing the tomatoes.
Robert	Initially wanted to examine how the (**24**) _____ of soil affects plant growth, but due to a late start he switched to the growing techniques used by apple farmers.	* The apple project had better success due to the later (**25**) _____. * Robert visited many apple growers near his parents' house.

Questions 26 – 30

Complete the sentences in the notes below.

Write **NO MORE THAN TWO WORDS AND/OR A NUMBER** from the listening for each answer.

Projects <u>MUST</u> be submitted as a (**26**) _____ to Professor Evans by the 28th February and by email to Mrs. Roberts by the (**27**) _____. Mrs. Roberts' email address is in the course literature, website and on the dept. noticeboard.

Word limit is increased this year by (**28**) _____ words (now 10,000, not including the (**29**) _____).

Prof. Evans' advice should stop projects from failing, but if they aren't good enough, the failing student will not (**30**) _____. The project can be redone (or a new one done) the next year.

PART 4   Questions 31 – 40

Questions 31 – 35

Choose the correct letter A, B, or C.

31   The Rorschach Test was initially based on

   A   how schizophrenics see things differently.

   B   schizophrenics self-analysis of themselves.

   C   observation of the schizophrenic child of a well-known psychologist.

32   The Rorschach Test uses

   A   a unique method in how it assesses people.

   B   a common method to assess people.

   C   a method that is nowadays very infrequently administered to assess people.

33   The Rorschach ink blots are

   A   first shown to subjects the day before the test.

   B   first shown to subjects an hour before the test.

   C   not supposed to be ever made public before the test.

34   The accuracy of the Rorschach Test

   A   has been demonstrated through careful experimentation.

   B   is now largely discredited.

   C   is widely used in the United States.

35   Interpretation of the Rorschach Test's results

   A   is still disputed among psychologists and psychiatrists using the test.

   B   is now universally done using the Exner Comprehensive System.

   C   are often confirmed using modern personality tests.

Questions 36 – 40

Complete the sentences below.

*Write **NO MORE THAN TWO WORDS** from the listening for each answer.*

36   In the Exner Comprehensive System, the structural summary results are meant to demonstrate _____ associated with the different responses given.

37   The rigidity of method used when delivering the Rorschach Test is supposed to keep _____ in results to a minimum.

38   The person delivering the Rorschach Test will rarely provide any _____ to the test taker.

39   Nowadays, the tests are recorded, but in the past, a particular _____ was created for people to write notes during the Rorschach Test.

40   Efforts are made to stop test takers becoming _____ or distracted, as this can create unreliable results.

READING

SECTION 1   Questions 1 – 14

Questions 1 – 8

The text on the following page has five descriptions of courses available at StudyWorld.

Which course description mentions the following information?

*Write the correct letter, **A - E**, in boxes **1 – 8** on your answer sheet.*

1   This course is the cheapest one offered at StudyWorld.

2   Most graduates in this subject find a job immediately.

3   This subject does not have to be studied full-time.

4   Teachers in this subject have worked in the field themselves.

5   Students in this subject must take part in a temporary work experience placement.

6   Students can access specific language assistance on this course.

7   Graduates in this subject have previously found jobs on board ships.

8   Students studying this course do not have to attend the StudyWorld college in person.

StudyWorld - *Courses to help you grow*

Here at StudyWorld, we have a variety of different courses with different demands. Many of our courses lead our students to a new job and career.

A   Design

This full-time course is based at our main campus. We have superbly equipped studios that provide top of the range computer software and hardware, outstanding printing resources, a photography workshop with darkroom, a studio for fashion and fabrics and fine arts, and traditional processing resources for photography. You'll be taught by lecturers who are art and design experts, with experience in creative industries. They really know their stuff, so you'll get lots of hints and tips about working in this sector.

B   Hair and Beauty

Our full-time courses in hairstyling and make-up for the media and entertainment industries take place in our specialised on-campus training studios, where all our students benefit from the experience of our skilled and motivated teaching team. There are lots of possibilities for jobs in hairdressing or beauty, and some of our past students have even gone on to become entrepreneurs with their own beauty studios. Our courses have led to a variety of rewarding jobs as hair stylists, beauticians, colour experts or salon managers and our students have ended up working in spas, 5-star resorts and on cruise liners. There's a lot of variety and the skills you will acquire can give you the opportunity to travel widely.

C   Hospitality and Catering

Working in the hospitality sector can give you the chance to work all around the world and with over 300 hotels and restaurants in the locality, there are lots of work prospects near the college, too. Some of our students go on to jobs in the best hotels in the world. This is a two-year full-time or three-year part-time course, with three months in an appointment at a hotel or restaurant. We always have many overseas students on this course and so students have access to special English support services if needed.

D   Sport and Fitness

It doesn't matter whether our students want to study fitness or specific sports coaching, our courses will provide them with what they need to move forward. 95% of our graduating students move from college to a job immediately and this more than anything shows how good our courses are. We have brand new facilities, equipped with the latest kit and our instructors are all familiar with the latest in coaching and training methods. Studying sport and fitness with us is also not all about the work. There are lots of sporting opportunities to exploit and the college raises teams in football, rugby, netball and cricket amongst others.

E   Media

Our full-time media course is completely taught and assessed online and students are free to choose how they study. As long as assignments are completed on time and they contribute to discussion forums and live room discussions, students can work at their own pace and where they choose. Because of this course's teaching and assessment structure, its fees are considerably less than all our other courses.

Questions 9 – 14

*Complete each sentence with the correct ending (**A - I**) below.*

*Write the correct letter (**A - I**) in boxes **9 - 14** on your answer sheet.*

9   The Kenton Job Centre is a service that used to

10   Part of the job of a personal advisor is to

11   Young disabled people are entitled to

12   Interview skills can be improved if candidates

13   Local businesses can find employees quickly and easily if they

14   People taking part in the Steps to Success programme

A   sign an out-of-work declaration every two weeks.

B   ensure people who receive unemployment benefit are fulfilling their responsibilities.

C   ask the consultants in the Kenton Job Centre Plus Office for advice.

D   take part in the Training for Success programme when older.

E   find training so that they can find new jobs.

F   be a combination of different services.

G   pass on their requirements to the Job Centre.

H   keep collecting any previously authorised financial assistance from the government.

I   are not responsible for being unemployed.

The Kenton Job Centre

The Kenton Job Centre is a part of the Department of Work and Pensions. It has taken over from the Employment Service, which ran the previous Kenton Work Agency, Benefits Agency and Social Security office.

The Kenton Job Centre provides employment and benefit services for people of working age. Personal advisors offer support and advice in your job search along with training provisions and benefit guidance. Whilst giving support to the unemployed, the personal advisors are also required to ensure that those claiming unemployment benefits are performing their obligations.

If you're a young person and you're thinking about entering the job market, then we may have some programs of interest for you:

The Youth Employment Scheme Work Experience Programme offers young people aged between 18 and 24 a period of work experience lasting between 2 and 8 weeks. Work experience will allow young people the chance to try tasks and experiences within a real workplace setting. Work experience can improve a young person's chances of finding work by developing employability skills and self-confidence. Participation is entirely voluntary and participants will retain their entitlement to benefit. Participants will also, where eligible have their travel and childcare costs reimbursed.

In addition young people can access the Training for Success programme. This is designed for young people aged 16 – 17, with extended eligibility up to age 22 for persons with a disability. The formal, accredited training, up to level 2, provides young people with the professional and technical skills, as well as the personal and behaviour skills required to progress to further or higher education, or employment in their chosen field of work.

If you need help writing your CV, interview tips or maybe you could do with improving your literacy or numeracy skills, speak to the consultants in the Kenton Job Centre Plus Office, who will be happy to advise you. You'll also find the touch screen, interactive job points very helpful in your search for employment.

Kenton Job Centre also offers assistance to Kenton employers. By informing the centre of their employee needs, the centre can find suitable candidates for the posts and employers are able to fill their vacancies quickly and successfully. Employers wishing to take advantage of this free service should contact our Employer Services Manager by email. Employers searching for a new employee should provide a job description, including required hours and offered salary/wages. The email address is available on the Contact Us page of our website.

Many people today want to work from home and online jobs could be the perfect solution for you. The Kenton Job Centre offers tips and advice to help you work online and earn a decent income, avoid work from home tricks and maximise your earning potential.

People having trouble finding work can use our Steps 2 Success programme. Participants will be assigned a liaison officer who will provide them with support to achieve their jobs goals. The liaison officer will help participants by discussing their job goals, previous work experience and individual circumstances, agreeing upon a personal 'Employment Plan', which will set out what will be done to help them get a job, and agreeing the in-work support available to help them stay in work when they find a job. While taking part in Steps 2 Success, participants will continue to receive any Social Security benefits they are entitled to.

SECTION 2   Questions 15 – 27

Questions 15 – 20

Complete the flow chart below.

Write **NO MORE THAN TWO WORDS** from the text for each answer.

Write your answers in boxes **15 – 20** on your answer sheet.

Our Company's Complaints Procedure

1. Speak with all the people involved to find an amicable solution.

↓

2. Contact your (**15**) _____, who will also try and reach a resolution.

↓

3. Make the complaint in writing to someone in senior management (see the (**16**) _____ for details on whom to write to). Explain the problem, what has already been done and what you think should happen. Don't forget to write your (**17**) _____.

↓

4. The company grievance procedure will now begin. The senior manager will write to you within 24 hours saying what will happen. He/she will email his/her decision within a week, which can be accepted or rejected.

↓

5. You can appeal to the general manager, who will set up a (**18**) _____, at which you can make your case. You can be accompanied by someone of your choosing. The general manager and two other senior managers will consider the issue and you will be emailed within a week with the decision, which can be accepted or rejected.

↓

6. You can appeal to the company director, who might refer the case to an impartial (**19**) _____, whose decision must be accepted by the company and employee.

↓

NB: It's best that you keep a (**20**) _____ of the procedure.

Page 41

Making a Complaint

From time to time, we have employees who have the need to make a complaint about something that happens here at work. This is something that we take very seriously and so we have created a process that you can follow, so that you know what to do if there is something that you need to complain about. Issues that may cause grievances could include terms and conditions of employment, health and safety, work relations, bullying and harassment, new working practices or organisational changes and discrimination.

First of all, it's usually best to deal with a complaint informally. If you feel you can, speak to the person or people who are involved and try and work out an amicable solution. If that does not work, then a further stage can be tried. Speak to your line manager (if the line manager is involved, speak to the line manager above him or her) and explain. He or she will try and resolve the problem with the people involved. We find that nearly all the problems within our company get solved with these informal procedures.

If the above two strategies do not work, you must begin the formal process of making a complaint. Our complaint procedure requires that a complaint should be made in writing and submitted to a member of the senior management. These people are clearly indicated on the company website. Employees should make clear the nature of their complaint, what they have already done informally to solve the problem and what would be their preferred solution. Employees must also supply their company email address.

Once an official complaint has been made, the company grievance procedure goes into operation. The senior manager will review the complaint and write an email to the employee who complained before the end of twenty-four hours. The senior manager will explain how he or she will handle the complaint. Before the end of a week, the senior manager will write an email again with his decision. The employee can choose to accept or reject this decision.

If the employee rejects the decision, he or she can appeal to the general manager, who will have been previously made aware of the complaint. The appeal should again be done in writing. The general manager will instigate a complaints meeting, where the employee can give his position verbally and in writing. Employees have the right to have with them a companion at a complaints meeting. The companion may be a fellow worker (i.e. another of the employer's workers), an official employed by a trade union or a workplace trade union representative, as long as they have been certified in writing by their union has having had experience. The complaints meeting will ensure an open discussion of the issues and give the employee a chance to say how they think the problem can be resolved. The general manager and two other senior managers will listen and discuss the issue. Again, within a week, the general manager will send an email with the decision.

If the employee still does not accept the decision, he or she can appeal again to the company director. If the director feels the appeal has merit, the case can be referred to an independent mediator. The employee and company must agree in writing before the mediation meeting to abide by the mediator's decision.

This is the end of our complaints procedure.

The managers involved are required to keep a written record of what happens during any complaint procedure. It is advised that employees do the same.

Questions 21 – 27

Complete the sentences below.

*Write **NO MORE THAN TWO WORDS** from the text for each answer.*

*Write your answers in boxes **21 - 27** on your answer sheet.*

21   Using a _____ can help workers keep their knees and hips aligned.

22   Workers who _____ their legs at their computers can suffer from difficulties with how they stand.

23   Workers should think about buying a _____, so that their computer screen is at eye level.

24   Sitting in an awkward posture over _____ can cause muscles to become overly tense.

25   Workers should move their _____ to one side when they are frequently using the mouse.

26   Stopping bright sunlight getting through the windows can reduce _____ on workers' eyes from the computer screens.

27   Using _____ may result in workers putting their heads in awkward positions too often.

Using your Computer Safely at Work

As we use computers here a lot in our company, we are very well aware that misuse of these devices can cause problems for the users. Computer workstations or other equipment can be associated with repetitive strain injuries (RSI's) in the neck, shoulder, back or arms, as well as with fatigue and eyestrain.

Support your back. Avoid back pain by adjusting your chair so that your lower back is properly supported. A correctly adjusted chair will reduce the strain on your back. Make sure you have one that is easily adjustable, so that you can change the height, back position and tilt. Have your knees level with your hips. You may need a footrest for this.

Adjust your chair. Adjust your chair height so that you can use the keyboard with your wrists and forearms straight and level with the floor. This can help prevent RSI's. Your elbows should be by the side of your body, so that the arm forms an L-shape at the elbow.

Rest your feet on the floor. Your feet should be flat on the floor. If they're not, ask if you can have a footrest, which lets you rest your feet at a level that's comfortable. Don't cross your legs, as this can cause posture-related problems.

Place your screen at eye level. Your screen should be directly in front of you. A good guide is to place the monitor about an arm's length away, with the top of the screen roughly at eye level. To achieve this, you may need to get a stand for your monitor. If the screen is too high or too low, you'll have to bend your neck, which can be uncomfortable.

Use the company masseur. Many of our workers remain for too long when they are at their computers. Consequently, there are particular muscles that will become tense when contracted in unnatural positions for extended periods. In order to deal with this problem, the company has a masseur visiting our offices regularly and she can be booked for free using the appropriate shared document. Massages are fifteen minutes and no employee should book in advance more than one session a week unless there are spaces on the day of a visit.

Using the keyboard. Leave a gap of about 100mm - 150mm at the front of the desk to rest your wrists between bouts of typing. Your wrists should be straight when using a keyboard. Keep your elbows vertical under your shoulder and right by your side. Some people like to employ a rest to keep their wrists straight and aligned with the keys.

Keep your mouse close. Position and use the mouse as close to you as possible. A mouse mat with a wrist pad may help to keep your wrist straight and avoid awkward bending. If you are not using your keyboard, push it to one side if using the mouse a lot.

Avoid screen glare. Your screen should be as free of this as possible. If it's on your screen, hold a mirror in front of it to identify the cause. Position the monitor to avoid the effects of overhead lighting and sunlight. If necessary, pull blinds across the windows and replace ceiling lighting with table lights. Adjusting the contrast can make it much easier to use.

Eye-related problems. People with bifocals may find difficulties with computer work, as it's important to be able to see the screen easily without having to raise or lower your head uncomfortably. If you can't work comfortably with them, you may need a different type of glasses.

SECTION 3   Questions 28 – 40

Read the following passage and answer Questions 28 – 40.

The World's Highest Bridges

A   The Siduhe River Bridge

Located about eighty kilometres south of the famous Three Gorges region of the Yangtze River in China's mountainous Hubei Province, the Siduhe suspension bridge is just one of several amazing structures on the last 483 kilometre link of the 2,175 kilometre long West Hurong highway that now connects Shanghai on the Pacific coast with the cities of Chongqing and Chengdu in the west. With a roadway 496 metres above the water, the Siduhe River Bridge is, as of 2014, the highest bridge in the world. One unique aspect of The Siduhe River Bridge's construction relates to its extreme height, remoteness and inaccessibility. Due to all this, the building engineers decided to experiment and, instead of using a blimp or helicopter to drag the initial pilot link across the gorge, they used a rocket.

B   The Hegigio Gorge Suspension Bridge

Located deep in the Southern Highlands Province of Papua New Guinea is the Hegigio Gorge Suspension Bridge, the highest pipeline bridge in the world. Some may argue that the Hegigio Gorge Bridge is not a true bridge, since it was not built for people, but for an oil pipeline. The bridge is a major component of the Southeast Mananda oil field infrastructure, an inaccessible expanse of oil that was discovered in 1991. The small size of the field and the extremely remote, jungle terrain made it a difficult petroleum project to undertake with many technical obstacles to overcome, the bridge being one of them. During construction, the north side of the bridge was difficult to reach, since there was no road access in place as there was on the south side. The first two hawsers were strung across by a helicopter, while successively thicker hawsers were then winched across. Another construction hurdle came from the harsh climate, which even today can be problematic to the operation of the pipeline. One oddity of the bridge is that there is no pedestrian walkway on the bridge. If necessary, personnel access for maintenance is made possible by a trolley that rides along two rails.

C   The Baluarte River Bridge

The Baluarte River Bridge is not only the highest bridge in North America, but the highest cable-stayed bridge in the world, surpassing the Millau Viaduct in France. It is the crown jewel of the greatest bridge and tunnel highway project ever undertaken in North America. The old road between the Pacific coast and the interior of Mexico is known as the "Devil's Backbone", and the road that created a safer and more direct route necessitated seven very high bridges and sixty-one tunnels; the Baluarte River Bridge is the highest of the bridges. Construction presented several problems. Firstly the foundations were carved directly into solid basalt, so extensive excavation works were needed. Secondly, the geographical location of the site required the construction of 25 kilometres of temporary roads. These location problems posed a big challenge.

D   The Balinghe River Bridge

With a height of 370 metres from deck to water, the Balinghe River bridge is the second highest bridge in China. It is unique for having the second longest span length with a distance between towers of 1088 metres. The reason why Balinghe River Bridge has this unusual span size relates to the luck that the Chinese associate with the number 8, which sounds like the Mandarin word for "prosperity". The bridge was meant to be a concrete beam bridge, but the lack of sand suitable for concrete in the area made this plan too expensive, as sand would have had to be transported to the building site. As a result, a suspension bridge was constructed, which is an excellent type of bridge to build across a large gap. The Balinghe River Bridge has two towers, which are easily supported by the main steel cables that curve from one tower to the other. The curving main steel cables also hold other cables (each is known as a suspender), which go down from the main steel cables to the road deck. It is unusual in that, at each end, the main steel cables continue into the ground and are attached to a concrete anchor that provides extra stability and support. Another peculiarity of the bridge is that, as it is situated between two mountain ranges, there is frequent cloud cover, which sometimes makes it appear to be floating among the clouds.

E   The Chenab River Bridge

There is probably no other natural barrier on earth that has been more formidable to railway engineers than the Himalayan mountain range that stretches across northern India. When construction began on the Chenab River Bridge, the engineers experienced extensive delays due to difficult geology, access problems, tunnel excavation difficulties and labour disputes. The bridge is not yet open, but, when it is, it will be the most expensive stretch of India's 64,374 kilometre railway network. The Chenab River Bridge will have busy traffic, as it is located fewer than sixteen kilometres north of the busy tourist town of Katra, which, due to its proximity to the Vaishno Devi, is the second most visited religious shrine in India. Being in Kashmir, the Chenab River Bridge is also very near the conflict area between India and Pakistan. For this reason, there is a constant armed guard present at the bridge and this will also remain after completion.

Questions 28 – 36

The text above has five descriptions of some of the highest bridges in the world.

Which description mentions the following information?

*Write the correct letter, **A - E**, in boxes **28 – 36** on your answer sheet.*

28   This bridge has protection 24 hours a day.

29   People can't walk across this bridge.

30   Due to this bridge's location, there were problems sending the first line across the expanse this bridge had to cover.

31   The construction plans for this bridge were changed because there wasn't enough of a certain building material.

32   This bridge was built as part of a network replacing a more dangerous road.

33   This bridge is only used to carry a pipe.

34   The length of part of this bridge is because of a national superstition.

35   The first cables to cross the expanse the bridge had to cover were taken by helicopter.

36   The construction of this bridge is not yet finished.

Questions 37 and 38

Label the diagram below.

*Write **NO MORE THAN THREE WORDS** from the text for each answer.*

*Write your answers in boxes **37 and 38** on your answer sheet.*

The Balinghe River Bridge

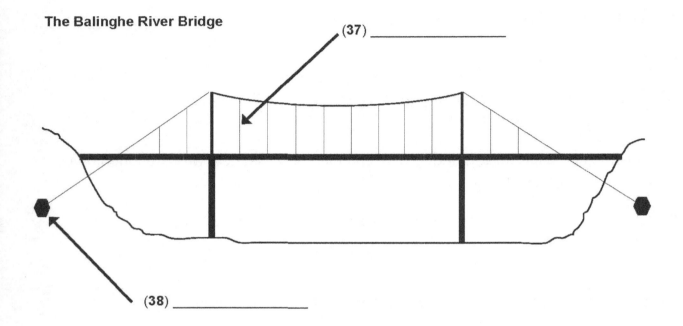

(37) _____

(38) _____

Questions 39 and 40

Do the following statements agree with the information given in the text?

*In boxes **39 and 40** on your answer sheet write:*

TRUE	*if the statement agrees with the information*
FALSE	*if the statement contradicts the information*
NOT GIVEN	*if there is no information on this*

39   The weather affects how at least one of the bridges is used.

40   Two of the bridges share the same architect.

WRITING

WRITING TASK 1

You should spend about 20 minutes on this task.

A friend of yours recently gave you a nice birthday present.

Write a letter to your friend. In your letter,

- **thank her for the present and say why you particularly like it**
- **describe some other presents that you received**
- **explain some of the things you did on your birthday**

You should write at least 150 words.

*You do **NOT** need to write any addresses. Begin your letter as follows:*

Dear Sarah,

WRITING TASK 2

You should spend about 40 minutes on this task.

Write about the following topic:

Some people believe that teaching music in schools is a vital part of growing up and the human experience, whilst others believe that teaching music in schools is a waste of time and resources.

Discuss both these views and give your own opinion.

Give reasons for your answer and include any relevant examples from your knowledge or experience.

You should write at least 250 words.

SPEAKING

PART 1

- Tell me about the outside of your house or apartment building.
- What can the outside of a building say about who lives there?
- What would you change to the outside of your house or apartment building?

Topic 1   Public Transport
- Do you use public transport? (Why/Why not?)
- How could public transport be improved where you live?
- Can you compare the bus and train as types of public transport?
- How can governments get people to use public transport more?

Topic 2   Films
- What kinds of films do you like and what kinds do you dislike?
- What can people learn from watching films?
- Is there a successful film industry in your country? (Why/Why not?)
- How have films changed since you started watching them?

PART 2

> Describe a memorable holiday that you once took.
> You should say:
> > where this holiday was
> > who you went with
> > what you did during this holiday
> and explain why this holiday was so memorable.

PART 3

Topic 1   The Holiday Industry
- Where do people from your country like to go on holiday?
- Why do people need holidays?
- Can you compare the holiday industry today with that of 30 years ago?
- What problems can tourists create in holiday resorts?

Topic 2   Moving to Another Country/Emigration
- Would you ever consider living permanently in another country other than your own? (Why/Why not?)
- Why do people choose to move to other countries?
- What problems do people face when they move to other countries?
- How do you think emigration patterns will change over the next 50 years?

PRACTICE TEST 3

LISTENING

PART 1   Questions 1 – 10

Questions 1 – 5

Complete Tom's Existing Customer Enquiry Form below.

Write **NO MORE THAN THREE WORDS AND/OR A NUMBER** *from the listening for each answer.*

Existing Customer Enquiry Form

Contract Number:	TR349573
Date of Birth:	12th March (**1**) _____
Zip Code:	85823
House Number:	(**2**) _____
Customer's Name:	Jennifer (**3**) _____
Home Telephone:	01934 (**4**) _____ 342
Monthly Bill Paid By:	(**5**) _____

Questions 6 – 10

Complete Jennifer's notes below.

Write **NO MORE THAN TWO WORDS AND/OR A NUMBER** *from the listening for each answer.*

Tom, the sales guy at R&N Mobile, said I would not get the extra (**6**) _____ of internet that I wanted, and he was able to issue a new contract, as the (**7**) _____ had not been activated yet. The new deal has no extra costs and also gives access to the fast TFR Network.

I can still terminate the contract as long as I do it (**8**) _____ days in advance. The price of US$(**9**) _____ per month has not changed.

If I want to get a new cell phone, I can order one on the website - Tom will send me the (**10**) _____ to the online store by email. I had to sign to reauthorize my payment.

PART 2   Questions 11 – 20

Questions 11 – 15

Choose **FIVE** letters, **A - O**.

Which of the following can be found in the Johnson Building?

A   Central coffee bar

B   The pizzeria

C   The French bistro

D   Asian street café

E   The main reception

F   The finance office

G   The maintenance team office

H   The first aid centre

I   The cinema

J   The doctor's surgery

K   The Fitness Area

L   The saunas

M   The steam rooms

N   The main swimming pool

O   The Internet café

Questions 16 – 20

Complete the table below.

*Write **NO MORE THAN THREE WORDS AND/OR A NUMBER** from the listening for each answer.*

Activity	Time	Notes
Water Park Complex	9 a.m. - 6 p.m.	£10 public. Reserved for holiday park (**16**) _____ from 9 a.m. to 12 noon.
Mini-golf	9 a.m. - 6 p.m.	All equipment supplied; groups play at (**17**) _____ intervals. No cost.
Jogging	8 a.m. or 5 p.m.	Morning jog easier - flat + (**18**) _____ km approx. in length. Afternoon jog harder - hillier + 6 km in length. Both runs begin with gentle (**19**) _____ and finish with stretching.
Levington Excursion	Minibus departs park at 1 p.m. + departs Levington at 5 p.m.	Costs £2; buy at reception or from the (**20**) _____; book early to avoid disappointment

PART 3   Questions 21 – 30

Questions 21 – 25

*Choose the correct letter **A, B, or C**.*

21   What is the subject of Professor Norris' seminar next week?

    A   History

    B   China

    C   The students' next essay

22   What is Alex's course about?`

    A   How wild boar were re-introduced in the UK

    B   How animals breed in different environments

    C   How foreign species of animal affect environments

23   What was most responsible for reducing the numbers of UK wild boar until they totally disappeared in the thirteenth century?

    A   Disease

    B   Too much hunting

    C   A royal order for their extermination

24   What was the main problem with farming wild boar in the UK in the 1970s?

    A   It did not make much money

    B   The animals kept escaping

    C   Hunters killed the animals

25   Why is the number of boar now probably more than 800?

    A   More and more boar have escaped from farms

    B   The escaped and released boar have bred

    C   The Forestry Commission has released more boar to ensure healthy bloodlines

Questions 26 – 30

Complete the summary below on the wild boars of the Forest of Dean.

Write **NO MORE THAN TWO WORDS** *from the listening for each answer.*

The Wild Boars of the Forest of Dean

The wild boars of the Forest of Dean are now officially wild animals and the local
(**26**) _____ is responsible for them.

Many locals say the high numbers of boars is not a problem. It's reported that the
(**27**) _____ will move the young away when they meet humans. Males are more
aggressive, but only dogs have been chased.

The Forestry Commission now regularly kills boars to control numbers, but animal
rights activists attempt to disrupt the (**28**) _____ working in the forest doing
this.

The forest cannot be closed on cull days and activists patrol the (**29**) _____
where they know the culls take place to protect the animals. The forest rangers are
upset, saying the boars create an imbalance in the forest. The rangers now try and
kill the wild boars on (**30**) _____ dates.

PART 4   Questions 31 – 40

Questions 31 – 34

Complete the notes below.

Write NO MORE THAN THREE WORDS AND/OR A NUMBER from the listening for each answer.

The New Zealand's Exclusive Economic Zone (EEZ)

New Zealand's EEZ is 5th largest in the world - covers approx. 3.9 million km^2.

New Zealand's EEZ's depth can be up to (**31**) _____ metres.

Underwater landscape of New Zealand's EEZ includes mountains, valleys, geysers + mudflats. Much marine life grows there.

Fishing can damage sea life, especially with bottom trawl or dredge equipment.
          Factors include: Type of seabed habitat
                                    The specialised (**32**) _____ used

Bottom-Trawling

Possibly the most destructive fishing type. Involves large nets being dragged over sea floor that take everything.

The unwanted species taken (called the (**33**) _____) are thrown back in sea, often dead or dying. This can be up to 90% of each trawl.

Conservationists claim sea floor life takes a long time to recover, if at all. This is disputed by (**34**) _____.

Questions 35 – 37

*Choose the correct letter **A, B, or C**.*

35   Part of New Zealand's fisheries management program is likened to

   A   similar initiatives in other countries.

   B   similar initiatives on land.

   C   similar initiatives that were not implemented in the past.

36   Most current BPA seabeds

   A   have never had trawlers operating there.

   B   have been carefully charted by the New Zealand Ministry of Fisheries.

   C   have been damaged by previous fishing.

37   Charted hydrothermal vents

   A   are difficult to locate for protection purposes.

   B   are key targets for the fishing industry.

   C   are closed to all fishing.

Questions 38 – 40

Complete the sentences below.

*Write **NO MORE THAN THREE WORDS AND/OR A NUMBER** from the listening for each answer.*

38   It's claimed that more than _____ per cent of the New Zealand EEZ has never been subject to bottom trawling.

39   Conservation critics of the New Zealand government claim that not all vulnerable _____ are protected.

40   The work of industrial trawlers also affects the _____ of smaller communities, as the catches of their fishermen also suffer.

READING

SECTION 1   *Questions 1 – 14*

Questions 1 – 9

*The text on the following page has six descriptions (**A - F**) of places to visit in the same area.*

Which description includes the following information?

*Write the correct letter (**A - F**) in boxes **1 - 9** on your answer sheet.*

1   This place will teach you skills to enjoy the facilities.

2   This place has something that can be visited temporarily.

3   You can get something to eat at this place.

4   You need to be a member to take advantage of all this place's possibilities.

5   You can watch a film at this place.

6   This place has just reopened.

7   Someone can show you round this place.

8   You can go online at this place.

9   This place has dedicated times for children.

Local Attractions to Visit

A   Caldor Castle

Caldor Castle is a great place for both adults and children. Children can run around the site, using their imagination to create old battles, and they can also begin to understand some history and its significance. Adults can learn about the importance of Caldor Castle and its varied history. See too in the dungeon the famous collection of weapons from the past. Guided tours available at 11 a.m. daily.

B   Chaffyn Beach

Whether it's sunny or rainy, Chaffyn Beach is a wonderful place to visit. In good weather, you can sit, sunbathe and swim or, in poor weather, it's a great place to go for a long walk to look at the spectacular sight of the sea, sky and the rain. Just off the beach next to the car park, there's a snack café that serves cool or hot drinks and hot and cold meal options every day.

C   The Motor Museum

Here you can learn about the history of driving and cars in a variety of interactive ways. With over 300 vehicles from the past to the present, you can see how the internal combustion engine changed the Earth from a place reliant on the horse to the mechanised world that we know today. Visitors will be able to enjoy a variety of the exhibits and can also enjoy the hourly film on the history of motor transportation that's shown in The Visitors Centre.

D   Icicles Ice Rink

Even if it's summer, Icicles Ice Rink will let you practice your skating skills on their giant ice surface. Full rental services are available for skating boots if you don't have your own. Icicles is open every day from nine a.m. until eleven p.m. On Saturday mornings there are special kids sessions from opening time until midday. If you've never done it before, coaching is available from the team of instructors. Call in advance to reserve an instructor, as they're always booked up.

E   The Fossil Museum

Step back millions of years into the past at the fossil museum. Recently back in business after renovation, the museum has a wide range of exhibits from the local area and from different places around the world. Right now, there is a special short-term exhibit on the famous *Tyrannosaurus rex* from the New York Natural History Museum. Children in particular will be amazed at the real-life dinosaur reconstructions and descriptions of these giant beasts.

F   The Main City Public Library

If you fancy just some peace and quiet and an undisturbed place to find and read a book, the Main City Public Library could be for you. With thousands of titles to find (and borrow if you're a registered reader), you'll be sure of finding something of interest. DVD's are also available for rental for registered readers. The library also has a range of computers connected to the internet, which anyone can use. These are not subject to reservation and are available on a first come first served basis. Computers may be used for one hour only, unless there is no one waiting to use one.

Questions 10 – 14

Complete the sentences below.

Write **NO MORE THAN ONE WORD** *from the text for each answer.*

*Write your answers in boxes **10 - 14** on your answer sheet.*

10   The price of a discount card depends on how old applicants are, as well
      as on their _____.

11   It's not possible to buy a discount card from a _____.

12   A _____ does not need to be supplied if the discount card is bought at a
      Blue Line office.

13   Card holders who _____ their cards online can obtain free replacements if
      the cards have been stolen.

14   Suitable _____ is always a good idea and not included in Blue Line vacation
      offers.

Blue Line Coaches
Bus Discount Card

Blue Line Coaches have buses regularly servicing the whole of Canada. If you travel a lot on your own or with your family, you might find that our special discount card can save you lots of money. We have thousands of people who take advantage of the discount card to travel more cheaply to visit friends, go to sports games, go to college and go on vacation.

Our discount card is available to anyone, though its price depends on the age and status of the person:

Under 18's	$50
Under 25's and full-time students	$70
Over 60's	$70
Others	$100

Our discount card is valid for one year from the date of purchase, but if you know that you will be doing lots of traveling, why not buy a three-year discount card? This costs 30% less than the cost of a one-year card and therefore will save you up to $30! Special deals are always available for family travel. Ask at any of our offices for our current offers.

The discount card can be bought at any of our offices around the country or online. Please note that you cannot buy the discount card on the buses themselves; a driver can only issue standard price travel tickets on the buses. All applications must be accompanied with a completed application form (also available at our offices or online) and a document that shows proof of age (for example, birth certificate, passport or driving licence). If you buy your discount card in person, you don't need to provide a photo, as this can be done at any of our offices.

If you're over 25 and a full-time student, you will need to provide proof of your current studies. This can be either your student photo card, stamped by your place of study, or a signed letter from your place of study, which must also be accompanied by a stamp. All Internet applications will need scans of supporting documentation and a digital passport-style photo.

After purchase of your discount card, we strongly recommend that you register your card online on our website. This means that if your card is misplaced or subject to theft, it can be replaced free of charge and others will not be able to use your missing card. Lost or misplaced cards should be reported to the police and a report including stamp should be obtained. This will help stop fraud, if people misuse your missing card.

Our discount card doesn't only save you money on bus travel. It can save you money with our partners too – various sports centres, cinemas, theaters, restaurants and hotels all offer discounts on production of your Blue Line discount card. Also, make sure you regularly visit our Rewards section on our website, where you will find up-to-date details of special offers that can be achieved with our discount card.

We have recently expanded our vacation offers to include some US cities. Recent additions include various destinations in Alaska, Chicago, Seattle, Portland, Boston and New York. Our packages include travel, accommodation and full board. The Blue Line discount card can also be used to gain attractive deals on selected holiday offers. See our website for current deals and special offers. Travellers are always advised to take out appropriate insurance when going on any foreign travel.

SECTION 2   *Questions 15 – 27*

Questions 15 – 21

Do the following statements agree with the information given in the text?

*In boxes **15 – 21** on your answer sheet write:*

TRUE	*if the statement agrees with the information*
FALSE	*if the statement contradicts the information*
NOT GIVEN	*if there is no information on this*

15   Some stress at work can lead to improved motivation.

16   Half of all illnesses related to people's workplace originate with stress.

17   The strong emotional reaction produced by a significant distressing episode is not typically a long-term phenomenon.

18   Hayworth Industries have a local GP who will advise people on work-related stress.

19   People shouldn't start doing anything new away from their place of employment if they feel stressed, as it will overwhelm them.

20   Hayworth Industries have stress workshops at lunchtimes, where staff can get advice on work-related stress.

21   Some staff at Hayworth Industries will know how to help colleagues with stress.

Hayworth Industries - Beat Stress

Here at Hayworth Industries, we're exceedingly proud of our workforce and everyone's work ethic and dedication to the company. We do recognise, however, that people sometimes expect too much of themselves. Some pressure at one's place of employment can act as an incentive, but when it becomes excessive, it can eventually lead to work-related stress. According to the government, last year 428,000 people reported work-related stress at a level they believed was making them ill. That's forty per cent of all employment-related sickness. Stress is not always work-related, but it can often affect your work. Sometimes after experiencing a traumatic event that is especially frightening — including personal or environmental disasters, or being threatened with an assault — people have a strong stress reaction to the event. Fierce emotions, jitters, sadness, or depression may all be part of this normal and usually temporary reaction to the stress of an overwhelming event.

- If you have a stress-related problem, physical activity can get you in the right state of mind. Exercise won't make your stress vanish, but it will reduce some of the emotional intensity that you're feeling, clearing your thoughts and enabling you to deal with your problems more calmly.

- A good support network of colleagues, friends and family can ease your work troubles and help you see things in a different way. Talking things through with a friend or colleague will also help you find solutions to your problems.***

- Set aside time for yourself. The extra hours in the workplace mean that people aren't spending enough time doing things that they really enjoy.

- Good time management means quality work rather than quantity. Working smarter means prioritising your work, concentrating on the tasks that will make a real difference to your work. Leave the least important tasks to last.

- It's important to avoid unhealthy stress management. Don't rely on alcohol, smoking and caffeine as your ways of coping. Men more than women are likely to do this. It might provide temporary relief, but it won't make the problems disappear.

- Learn to recognise the physical effects of stress and do something about it before it makes you really ill and beware of work stress spilling over into other areas of your life.

- Setting yourself goals and challenges, whether at work or outside, such as learning a new language or a new sport, helps to build confidence. That in turn will help you deal with stress. By continuing to learn, you become more emotionally resilient as a person. It arms you with knowledge and makes you want to do things rather than be passive.

- Family-related stress can be particularly distressing. This can affect you, your partner and your children. Because of their level of development, children and adolescents often struggle with how to cope well with stress. Youth can be particularly overwhelmed when their stress is connected to a traumatic event like a family loss, school problems, or violence. You might need time to take steps to provide stability and support that help young people feel better.

*** Whatever the source of your stress, speak to your line manager. They all have training in assisting our workforce with any stress-related problems.*

Questions 22 – 27

*Complete each sentence with the correct ending (**A - I**) below.*

*Write the correct letter (**A - I**) in boxes **22 - 27 on** your answer sheet.*

22   How much leave a worker is due

23   An employee should consult his contract to see if he

24   An employer who is given a leave request

25   When employees are entitled to take a public holiday

26   An employee who is working on a public holiday

27   Leave taken by a worker for looking after an ill son or daughter

A   is based on where the worker lives in Australia.

B   is permitted to transfer unused leave days into the next statutory leave year.

C   is dependent on whether the worker is employed full-time or part-time.

D   is not influenced by whether the worker is on maternity leave or not.

E   is obliged to make the request for leave in writing.

F   is not necessarily entitled to a better rate of pay.

G   is allowed to refuse it if he provides the right amount of notice.

H   is part of the worker's leave allowance.

I   is always paid a preferential rate.

Australian Leave Entitlements

Employees can take leave or holiday for many reasons, including to go on a vacation, take advantage of a national holiday, because they are sick, or to take care of sick family members.

Annual Leave

Annual leave begins to build up as soon as a worker starts their job. An employer must usually tell their staff the dates of their statutory leave year as soon as they start working, e.g. it might run from 1 January to 31 December. Workers must take their statutory leave during this time. The leave year and leave entitlement is not affected by new parent or adoption leave; the employee still builds up holiday over these periods. If a worker does not take all his/her leave days owed to him/her in his/her leave year, he/she may be able to carry the leave over to the next year. How much leave a worker can carry over should be in the worker's contract. The general notice period for taking leave is at least twice as long as the amount of leave a worker wants to take (e.g. 2 days' notice for 1 day's leave), unless the contract says something different. An employer can turn down a leave request, but they must give as much notice as the amount of leave requested. If a worker has taken more leave than they're entitled to, their employer must not take money from their final pay unless it's been agreed beforehand in writing. The rules in this situation should be outlined in the employment contract, company handbook or intranet site. During their notice period the worker may be able to take whatever is left of their statutory annual leave. The only time someone can get paid in place of taking statutory leave (known as 'payment in lieu') is when they leave their job. Employers must pay for untaken statutory leave (even if the worker is dismissed for gross misconduct).

Public Holidays

Public holidays can be different depending on the state or territory you work in. It's important to know when public holidays are, because employees can get different entitlements on these days. An employee is entitled to public holidays depending on where they are based for work, not where they are working on the day of the public holiday. Employees get paid at least their base pay rate for all hours worked on a public holiday. Whether extra pay is due to a worker depends on the worker's contract, but this is not guaranteed. Employees don't have to work on a public holiday; however, an employer can ask an employee to work on a public holiday, if the request is reasonable. An employee may refuse a request to work if they have reasonable grounds.

Sick and Carer's Leave

Sick and carer's leave (also known as personal leave or personal/carer's leave) lets an employee take time off to help them deal with personal illness, caring responsibilities and family emergencies. You're allowed a reasonable amount of time off to deal with the emergency, but there's no set amount of time as it depends on the situation. Sick leave can be used when an employee is ill or injured. An employee may have to take time off to care for an immediate family or household member who is sick or injured or help during a family emergency. This is known as carer's leave, but it comes out of the employee's personal leave balance. There are no limits on how many times you can take time off for dependants. Your employer may want to talk to you if they think time off is affecting your work. If employees aren't given time off for dependants, their employer may allow them 'compassionate leave' - this can be paid or unpaid leave for emergency situations. Employees should check their employment contracts, company handbook or intranet for details about compassionate leave.

SECTION 3   *Questions 28 – 40*

Questions 28 – 35

*The text on the following pages has 8 paragraphs (**A – H**).*

Choose the correct heading for each paragraph from the list of headings below.

*Write the correct number, **i - x**, in boxes **28 - 35** on your answer sheet.*

i	Initial Discovery Rejected
ii	Ancient Use
iii	Manufacture
iv	A Dangerous Precedent
v	Aspirin Proved as a Heart Drug
vi	Unreliable Approaches to Research
vii	Side Effects
viii	Further Research Uncovers New Uses
ix	Extra Funding Allocated
x	Limitations

28	Paragraph A
29	Paragraph B
30	Paragraph C
31	Paragraph D
32	Paragraph E
33	Paragraph F
34	Paragraph G
35	Paragraph H

The History of Aspirin

Paragraph A

The Assyrians of the Sumerian period and the Egyptians of the same time recorded that willow could be used to alleviate pain. Of course, these observations were made long before the advent of modern evidence-based medicine, and therefore the use of willow in early medicine had its foundation in observational or anecdotal evidence. Although physicians from these times had no way of understanding the mechanism by which willow bark might relieve pain, this lack of understanding did not stop them from prescribing this relatively safe and helpful herbal remedy.

Paragraph B

In 1897, Felix Hoffman, a German chemist researching for a major pharmaceutical company, was able to modify salicylic acid to create acetylsalicylic acid, which was named aspirin. The company initially were not impressed with aspirin as a useful drug, preferring to explore the use of heroin as a cough remedy. Eventually, aspirin was more fully researched and its efficacy as a pain reliever was proved and then marketed. In this manner, an ancient herbal remedy became the wonder drug, aspirin.

Paragraph C

In the second half of the twentieth century, more scientific investigation led to reports that daily, low doses of aspirin could prevent heart attack and stroke. This finding was first reported by Lawrence Craven, a suburban general practitioner in Glendale, California. Unfortunately, Craven's work and analysis went largely unnoticed, and decades passed before his observations were verified by clinical trials. The cause of heart attack was a topic of particular interest to Dr. Craven. He was not a formally trained scientist, but he knew his limitations. Indeed, some of the most remarkable aspects of his papers are his humility and his repeated warnings that more rigorous scientific studies had to be conducted to prove his hypotheses. Despite the absence of control groups, Craven's studies had their basis in sound reasoning and in the observation of large numbers of patients.

Paragraph D

Craven's lack of rigor and scientific method led to his published papers going largely unnoticed and decades passed before his observations were verified by clinical trial. Most of Craven's writing is speculative and descriptive, lacking any statistics or formal presentation of data. Another reason why Craven's assertions were not taken seriously was that he published his papers in journals that were not respected by the scientific community.

Paragraph E

Since the publication of Craven's clinical observations, hundreds of clinical trials have tested aspirin's ability to prevent cardiovascular events, and it is now accepted that aspirin can prevent both coronary thrombosis and strokes. The later research studied how aspirin can reduce the risk of blood clots by stopping the part of blood known as platelets from sticking together. Usually platelets sticking together is a positive thing, as it stops people losing blood when they cut themselves. When it happens inside the body, it can cause a coronary thrombosis or stroke.

Paragraph F

Dr. Craven's observations suggested that aspirin completely prevented the chance of a heart attack. However, clinical trials have shown that, while aspirin significantly reduces the risk of heart attacks and strokes, it clearly is not universally protective. Craven himself recommended aspirin for heart attack prevention in men between forty-five and sixty-five, who were overweight and sedentary, factors known to lead to heart attacks. All of Craven's study patients were men, because part of his hypothesis was based on his observation that more men than women were suffering heart attacks. Also, although aspirin may be effective in preventing a stroke, it is important not to take aspirin when having a stroke. This is because strokes can have different causes. If a stroke is caused because of a blood clot in the brain, an aspirin may help. Some strokes, however, are caused by a burst blood vessel in the brain and this bleeding may get worse if an aspirin is taken due to its blood-thinning properties.

Paragraph G

Aspirin is generally a very safe drug. Like many drugs taken orally, it can cause some gastrointestinal irritation, but this is usually avoided if it is taken with food. It can also cause nausea, vomiting, heartburn and rashes, though these reactions are all fairly rare. High doses of aspirin can also cause a temporary hearing loss or a ringing in the ears, but this usually only occurs with large doses and is rare in any treatments with low doses. Of course, the one reason why aspirin is so effective with helping people ward off heart attacks and strokes is that it thins the blood. It should therefore not be taken if someone is having an operation, as any opening of the skin will bleed more freely than usual. Children should not usually take aspirin. It can help in some rare conditions, but potential risks to children's metabolism has forced doctors to only use it sporadically.

Paragraph H

Aspirin's chemical name is acetylsalicylic acid. It is made today by placing acetic anhydride and toluene in a mixing tank, before transferring the mixture to a reaction chamber, where salicylic acid is added and the chamber heated. After the chemical reaction has taken place, the mixture is cooled before filtration occurs. The exiting product is acetylsalicylic acid, which can then be converted to the form of aspirin that is required. Residue from filtration can be treated for a short while, before it can again be re-used in the process.

Questions 36 – 38

Do the following statements agree with the views of the writer of the text?

In boxes **36 - 38** on your answer sheet write:

YES	if the statement agrees with the writer's views
NO	if the statement doesn't agree with the writer's views
NOT GIVEN	if it is impossible to say what the writer thinks about this

36   Aspirin is more effective for a certain target age group.

37   Craven was annoyed by the initial lack of acceptance of his theories.

38   Aspirin is a useful first response for someone suffering from a stroke.

Questions 39 and 40

Label the diagram below.

Write **NO MORE THAN THREE WORDS** from the text for each answer.

Write your answers in boxes **39 and 40** on your answer sheet.

Aspirin Production

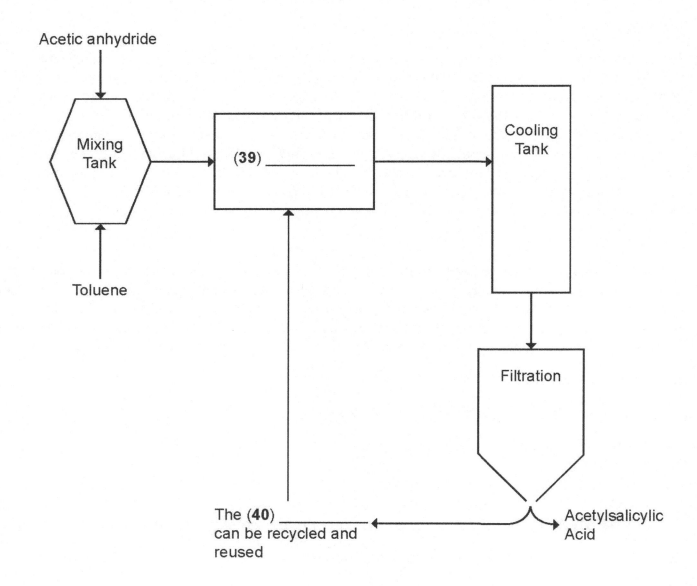

WRITING

WRITING TASK 1

You should spend about 20 minutes on this task.

You and your family have just come back from a holiday staying in a rented apartment overlooking the sea. The apartment was very unsatisfactory.

Write a letter of complaint to the manager of the agency from which you rented the apartment. In your letter,

- **give details of the things that were unsatisfactory**
- **explain the reactions of the members of your family**
- **ask the manager what he / she is going to do about the situation**

You should write at least 150 words.

*You do **NOT** need to write any addresses. Begin your letter as follows:*

Dear Sir / Madam,

WRITING TASK 2

You should spend about 40 minutes on this task.

Write about the following topic:

Many people believe in the idea of school children wearing a school uniform, but should teachers as well be required to conform to a dress code?

Give reasons for your answer and include any relevant examples from your knowledge or experience.

You should write at least 250 words.

SPEAKING

PART 1

- Tell me a little about your country.
- What are some of the advantages and disadvantages of living in your country?
- Where would you advise a visitor to your country to visit? (Why?)

Topic 1   Libraries
- Do people in your country go to libraries? (Why/Why not?)
- What function do libraries have in communities?
- Do you feel that using a library should be free?
- Do you think libraries are a thing of the past or do you think they have a future?

Topic 2   Sports
- Do you play any sports? (Why/Why not?)
- What sport would you/did you encourage your child to play?
- Why do you think people like to watch sports?
- What is your attitude to high risk/dangerous sports?

PART 2

Describe a memorable place that you have visited
You should say:
      where this place is
      when you first went there
      what you did there
and explain why this place is so memorable for you.

PART 3

Topic 1   Cities
- Do you prefer to live in a city or in the countryside? (Why?)
- What are the advantages of living in a big city?
- What are some of the problems of living in a modern city?
- How do you think cities will change in your country over the next 50 years?

Topic 2   The Environment
- Does your country suffer from pollution problems?
- How does your country's government deal with pollution?
- What do you feel is more important, the environment or people's standard of living? (Why?)
- Do you think overpopulation is an important environment issue?

PRACTICE TEST 4

LISTENING

PART 1   ***Questions 1 – 10***

Questions 1 – 5

Complete Jake's reservation change form below.

*Write **NO MORE THAN TWO WORDS AND/OR A NUMBER** from the listening for each answer.*

The Sutherland Hotel
Reservation Change Form

Reservation Number   EZT 486 978

Customer's Name: Mrs. Jane (**1**) _____

Address: (**2**) _____ Richmond Rise
                            Birkdale
                            Auckland

Postcode: 0626

Date of Birth: 14th (**3**) _____ 1985

Reservation Website Used: (**4**) _____

(**5**) _____ not charged by the website!

Questions 6 – 10

Complete Jake's summary email confirming the change in hotel reservation.

Write NO MORE THAN THREE WORDS AND/OR SOME NUMBERS for each answer.

Re: your reservation change

Dear Madam,

Thanks for your call. I have made the change you requested to your booking and I have summarised the information below:

The two adults in the booking have not changed. Two children have been added: Mark ((**6**) _____ years) + Max (eight years). The boys will have a twin room with no (**7**) _____. Original booking from Friday 22nd May - Wednesday 27th May. New booking from Saturday 23rd May - Wednesday 27th May.

Price changes: Adult booking 1 day fewer. Boys: Mark is charged the full rate; Max is charged the child rate. Old price NZ$1200; new price NZ$(**8**) _____ exactly.

The booking is held by a VISA card with the last four numbers 8537. Previous (**9**) _____ paid does not need to be increased.

(**10**) _____ is included for all guests in the booking.

Best wishes,
Jake

PART 2   *Questions 11 – 20*

Questions 11 and 12

*Answer the questions below. Write **NO MORE THAN THREE WORDS AND/OR A NUMBER** from the listening for each answer.*

11   When was the chocolate factory built?

12   How many full-time employees work at the factory?

Questions 13 – 15

Complete the flow chart describing the tour of the chocolate factory.
*Write **NO MORE THAN THREE WORDS** from the listening for each answer.*

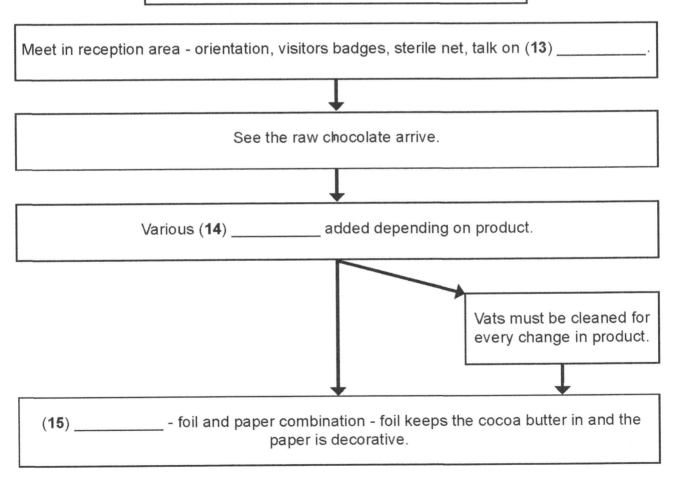

Chocolate Factory - Tour of Manufacturing Area

Meet in reception area - orientation, visitors badges, sterile net, talk on (13) _____ .

See the raw chocolate arrive.

Various (14) _____ added depending on product.

Vats must be cleaned for every change in product.

(15) _____ - foil and paper combination - foil keeps the cocoa butter in and the paper is decorative.

Questions 16 – 20

Complete the notes below on the second part of the talk on the tour of the chocolate factory. Write **NO MORE THAN ONE WORD AND/OR A NUMBER** *from the listening for each answer.*

Return to admin. area after the manufacturing tour:

    * a film on the history of chocolate
    * a brief (**16**) _____ on the company's marketing + sales strategies

Tasting

The (**17**) _____ will help you choose from all our products; (don't eat too much - especially children)

Administration

Individuals and Small Groups

One tour in morning starting at (**18**) _____ a.m.; one tour in afternoon starting at 2 p.m.

    Adults - $13
    Senior citizens - $9
    Children - $6

Larger and School Tours

    Adults - $ (**19**) _____
    Senior citizens - $9
    Children - $4 (accompanying school staff free)
    (these tours can be at any time, but must be booked in advance)

* All guides have police screening for working with children
* Free parking for cars and coaches
* Complete (**20**) _____ access
* Guide dogs welcome (but not in the manufacturing areas)

PART 3   Questions 21 – 30

Questions 21 – 25

Complete the tables below on Tina and Edward's course change situations.

Write **NO MORE THAN ONE WORD** from the listening for each answer.

Tina			
	Year 1 Subjects	Main Subject Now	New Main Subject Wanted
	History	History	Linguistics
	French		
	Linguistics		
Notes			
Misses linguistics in her 2nd year. Liked history, but finds she has to study too many (**21**) _____ she doesn't want to. Even with 3rd year (**22**) _____, she will still have too many compulsory things to study.			

Edward			
	Year 1 Subjects	Main Subject Now	New Main Subject Wanted
	History	History	Earth Sciences
	English		
	Earth Sciences		
Notes			
Studied Earth Sciences in year 1, as he wanted something different; had no problem in the 1st year. Likes History and English, but finds he has too many (**23**) _____ in these subjects. Did additional summer (**24**) _____ and discussed it with his family. In Earth Sciences, students are assessed by smaller assignments, (**25**) _____ and shorter exams.			

Questions 26 – 28

Choose **THREE** letters, **A - G**.

Which **THREE** people need to sign Edward's form so that he can change subject?

A   Professor Holden

B   Doctor Flynn

C   Mr Thomas

D   Professor Atkins

E   Mr Morton

F   Miss Morgan

G   Professor Evans

Questions 29 and 30.

Choose the correct letter **A, B, or C**.

29   Other than taking the forms to the registrar's office, Professor Holden says that the only other way to get the forms to the registrar's office is

    A   to give the completed forms to him.

    B   to email the completed forms.

    C   to post their completed forms.

30   The registrar's office is found

    A   on the third floor of the offices above the post office.

    B   on the third floor of the administrative building opposite the post office.

    C   on the second floor of the administrative building opposite the post office.

PART 4   Questions 31 – 40

Questions 31 – 34

Complete the notes and diagram related to the Great Artesian Basin below.

Write **NO MORE THAN THREE WORDS** from the listening for each answer.

The Formation of the Great Artesian Basin

Gondwana, a land mass created in the Triassic age, had a (**31**) _____ in its north west corner. Due to great movement of the earth over the next 100 million years, the ocean level rose and fell. The natural dip filled with water, which left deposits of
(**32**) _____ that created the impermeable stone strata that would hold the Great Artesian Basin's water reservoir.

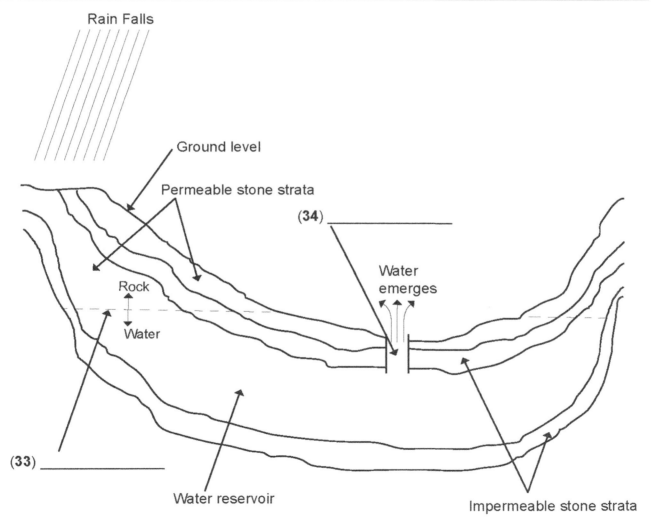

Questions 35 – 40

Complete the notes below. Write **NO MORE THAN THREE WORDS** *from the listening for each answer.*

---

* It's estimated 65,000,000,000 megalitres are in the Great Artesian Basin.
* It brings life to arid areas in Australia - various flora and fauna survive in these unique (**35**) _____.
* Water also gets into river systems helping them flow in dry times.
* Man-made bore holes create artesian wells - these support agriculture and (**36**) _____.

* Modern usage of the Great Artesian Basin has caused problems:
      Some wells and sources are dry.
      Some bore holes can't be turned off - wastes water and supports weeds + feral animals.
      95% of water from these running bore holes (**37**) _____ or soaks away.
      Many old bore holes badly made - water escapes.

* New strategy created to manage the water:
      Capping - putting lids on bores (water accessed by using a (**38**) _____).
      Piping - replaces channels / drains; water goes to (**39**) _____ preventing wastage.

* Strategy to protect water from the Great Artesian Basin is vital to all of Australia. If water from the Great Artesian Basin is lost...
      ... 70 towns would disappear.
      ... AUS$1 billion would be lost from the beef, wool and sheep industries.
      ... the effect on Australia's food production system would mean that more food would have to be imported (this would affect Australia's (**40**) _____ and whole economy).

READING

SECTION 1   Questions 1 – 14

Questions 1 – 6

Complete the sentences below.

Write **NO MORE THAN TWO WORDS** from the text for each answer.

Write your answers in boxes **1 - 6** on your answer sheet.

1   Using the washing machine where it's too cold can affect its controls and can damage its _____.

2   The installed _____ of the washing machine should be removed before the washing machine is first run.

3   It's important to ensure adequate _____ is provided under a washing machine.

4   Poorly attached drain lines can result in _____.

5   If the _____ is used properly in the washing machine, de-scaling should not be necessary.

6   How much laundry is put into the machine not only affects how much water is used, but also the _____.

Instructions for your New Washing Machine

• Keep these instructions in a safe place for future reference. Should the appliance be sold, transferred or moved, make sure the instruction manual accompanies the washing machine to inform the new owner as to its operation and features.

• Young children should not be allowed to touch the machine or play with its controls. They should be supervised when the machine is in operation. Older children may use the machine if they have been instructed how to use it and if they are aware of the dangers of misuse.

• Your new washing machine should not be installed in a place where temperatures may drop below 0° Celsius or the functioning of the electronic controls may not work properly and water hoses may burst or split. The washing machine should also not be installed in an outdoor environment, not even when the area is sheltered, because it may be very dangerous to leave it exposed to rain and thunderstorms.

• Before first use, ensure that the protective transit bars have been removed from the back of your new machine. If they are still there during operation, it can result in damage to your machine. Levelling your appliance correctly will provide it with stability and avoid any vibrations, noise and shifting during operation. If it is placed on a fitted or loose carpet, adjust the feet in such a way as to allow enough room for ventilation beneath the washing machine.

• Ensure that you carefully read the washing labels on all items to be washed in your new washing machine. These labels on your garments will help you to keep your garments looking their best. This will prevent any accidents happening to your possessions.

• If you leave your new washing machine for any length of time, make sure that you turn off the machine's stopcock.

• If the drain line of your new washing machine is placed in a wash basin, make sure that water can drain away fast enough to avoid flooding. Ensure too that the drain line is secure or the force of the water exiting it may dislodge its position, which also can result in flooding. Make sure there are no kinks or bends in the drain line. The length of any extension to the drain line must have the same diameter as the original and must not exceed 150 cm in length.

• Check all items placed into your new washing machine for coins, nails, paper, tissues and other similar things, as they may clog up or break the machinery.

• Correct use of detergent will avoid the need for descaling, but if it's necessary, it's important to use one of the suggested de-scaling agents given at the end of this booklet and follow the agent's instructions carefully.

• Any items pre-washed in solvent-based agents should be carefully rinsed in cold water before being washed in your new washing machine.

• The first time you use your new washing machine, make sure it's empty.

• Water and energy consumption are linked to the size of your laundry load. To exploit your new washing machine at its full potential, always fill your machine with the maximum dry load for the programme you have chosen.

Questions 7 – 11

Answer the questions below.

Write **NO MORE THAN THREE WORDS** *from the text for each answer.*

Write your answers in boxes **7 - 11** *on your answer sheet.*

7   Where does non-recyclable rubbish end up?

8   What should householders be careful not to leave in their bio-waste?

9   Where should rubbish bins be left for rubbish removal?

10   What will the bulky rubbish collectors not pick up?

11   How will people be able to spend their credit in the recycling rewards programme?

Re: Rubbish Collection in your Area

Dear Householder,

In order to help protect our environment, your local town council has set itself certain targets regarding rubbish collection and recycling. We hope to reduce the amount of non-recyclable waste that we send to landfill sites and increase recycling. In order to reach our targets, we ask householders to divide their rubbish up by type. We have delivered differently coloured rubbish bins with instruction to each house in the area. All you need to do is to put your rubbish into the correct bin and leave the bins out on the correct day for collection.

Collection Days for your Area

Bio-waste*	Every Wednesday
Glass and metal	Every other Thursday
Plastics	Every other Thursday
Non-recyclable waste	Every Friday

* Bio-waste is burned to generate power. Because of this, please ensure no plastic is in your bio-waste or the fumes from it burning will pollute the air.

Collections will take place before 10 a.m. Rubbish bins ought to be put out on the pavement the night before the collection, but they must be returned to your property within 24 hours.

The Community-recycling Centre

Sometimes people will have rubbish that they want to dispose of before a collection. Your local town council has a community-recycling centre, where most of your rubbish can be dropped off. Non-household waste can also be disposed of here, but a small charge will be applicable. Household waste comprises of the unwanted contents of the house that are not part of the house itself. Construction waste includes items from the repair or improvement of houses (e.g. DIY type waste), as well as waste created from landscaping or garden alterations. If you want to use the community-recycling centre, please take some identification with you to prove you live in the local area. This can include anything that displays your name and address.

Bulky Items

We will collect bulky household waste that will not fit into your bin. This service is free, but must be booked online in advance. You can book up to six household items per collection. If you have more than six items, you will need to book another collection once the first one is finished, or take the items to the council's Re-Use Centre. The bulky service does not collect any building waste. You can get rid of some materials free of charge at the council's Re-Use Centre, but there may be a fee for others.

Recycling Rewards Programme

Your local town council is also developing a local recycling rewards programme that will allow local residents to accrue reward points. These points can be used to join a local rebate scheme with residents able to redeem their rewards using prepaid cards. The scheme will involve ideas such as residents ensuring unused food goes to the homeless, rather than just being thrown away.

Questions 12 – 14

Do the following statements agree with the information given in the advertisement for Blackstone Solicitors?

In boxes 12 – 14 on your answer sheet write:

TRUE	*if the statement agrees with the information*
FALSE	*if the statement contradicts the information*
NOT GIVEN	*if there is no information on this*

12   Blackstone Solicitors has a fixed price of only £50 for the first meeting with one of their solicitors.

13   Blackstone Solicitors specialise in helping people move overseas.

14   New customers can take advantage of introductory offers.

BLACKSTONE SOLICITORS   *Do you need expert legal advice?*

Blackstone Solicitors will provide you with the highest
quality legal services at highly competitive prices.

Experts in conveyancing, wills, probate, power of attorney, migration and family law.

- Over 30 years experience
- Free initial consultation
- Nationwide and international service
- No hidden charges
- Discounts for over 65's
- 24-hour helpline

We can also provide teams to provide services related to corporate, private client, argument resolution, employment and property. We can guide businesses or individuals with regards to setting up businesses in this country and overseas and we can provide advice on hiring overseas staff, relocations, wealth management and taxation. Call us now or visit our website for more details. Repeat clients can take advantage of discounted rates.

www.blackstonesolicitors.com
0800 738 2435

SECTION 2   *Questions 15 – 27*

Questions 15 – 20

Complete the notes below.

*Write **NO MORE THAN THREE WORDS** for each answer.*

*Write your answers in boxes **15 - 20** on your answer sheet.*

New Zealand Business Structures

Sole Traders

The owner is the business, but can take on employees.
Owner wholly responsible for (**15**) _____, business operations and profits.
Good way to start due to less red tape - owner and business are the (**16**) _____.
Separate business account not needed (though keep financial records for 5 years).
A lot fewer administration payments (you can pay your own superannuation though).

Partnerships

2 or more people combine assets, and share profits and losses.
All aspects of a partnership summarised in a partnership agreement.
If a partner is (**17**) _____, the other is responsible for all debts.
Vital to create a (**18**) _____.

Companies

Separate from shareholders - creates limited liability (unless shareholder takes part in running the company and is doing so poorly).
Moneylenders often only offer loans when there is a personal guarantee.
Shareholder income is subject to different (**19**) _____.
Companies must declare various company details at the Companies Office.
Complications can arise when an owning member leaves the business; previously agreed (**20**) _____ can help with not having to dissolve the company.

Starting a Business in New Zealand - Types of Structures

Did you know there are a few different ways you can structure your business? It's possible to do business in New Zealand under one of three basic types of business structure. Each offers varying degrees of control and responsibility.

Sole Traders

If you're a sole trader, your business is built around you. The entire operation relies on you, but you can still employ others to help you. You're 100% accountable for your business' liabilities, but you also retain full control of the business and its profits. Many small business owners start out as sole traders, because sole traders aren't required to spend money following any formal or legal processes to establish their business, unlike companies. This is because sole traders and their businesses are considered to be the same legal entity. Being a sole trader, you don't require a separate business bank account, unlike a company structure. You can use your personal bank account but must keep financial records for at least five years. If you're a sole trader without employees, there's no obligation to pay payroll tax, superannuation contributions or workers' compensation insurance on income you draw from the business. You can choose to make voluntary superannuation contributions to yourself though.

Partnerships

A partnership is when two or more people or entities join together to pool their assets and divide the profits and liabilities in a business. They often bring different skills to the table and varying resources, with the division of profits and liabilities – in addition to individual roles and responsibilities – outlined in a partnership agreement. Individuals are liable for their own debts and you can also be liable for business debts incurred by your partners if they become insolvent. Because partnerships entail more than one person in the decision-making process, it's important to discuss a wide variety of issues up front and develop a partnership agreement. This should document how future business decisions will be made, including how the partners will divide profits, resolve disputes, change ownership (bring in new partners or buy out current partners) and how to dissolve the partnership. Although they are not legally required, they are strongly recommended and it is considered extremely risky to operate without one.

Companies

Companies are separate legal entities to their shareholders. This provides shareholders with limited liability from any of the business' debts beyond the value of their shares in the company. However, if a shareholder is involved in the running of the business (as a director, for example), and he or she is found to have traded recklessly, fraudulently or not in the company's best interests, they can still be made liable. Most financial lenders will also only give a business loan in exchange for a personal guarantee overriding limited liability. Shareholder dividends undergo taxation at a different rate to the company itself. All companies have to declare their director and shareholder details by registering for incorporation with the Companies Office. When an owning 'member' leaves a company, the business is dissolved and the members must fulfil all remaining legal and business obligations to close the business. The remaining members can decide if they want to start a new company or part ways. However, you can include provisions in your operating agreement to prolong the life of the company if a member decides to leave the business.

Questions 21 – 27

Do the following statements agree with the information given in the text?

In boxes 21 – 27 on your answer sheet write:

    TRUE   *if the statement agrees with the information*
    FALSE   *if the statement contradicts the information*
    NOT GIVEN   *if there is no information on this*

21   All company expenses can only be returned at the end of every three months.

22   Some reimbursement from the company could be classed and taxed as additional salary.

23   Employees can claim for food when staying at a hotel on company business.

24   Employees can only claim for using their car when the company cars are not available.

25   Employees can be paid back some money back on their own home Internet connection if they use it sometimes for work purposes.

26   Employees cannot be repaid taxi expenses for their customers when entertaining.

27   No expenses can be paid without production of the relevant receipt.

Company Expenses - Information for Employees

Expenses are paid back to employees every quarter. Fill out digitally the expenses form, which is available in the company forms section on the shared drive of your computer. Send the expenses form to your line manager by email. Take all the relevant receipts for your expenses and place them in an envelope, which you must give to your line manager. Make sure your name and date references are on the outside of the envelope. Please keep a digital copy of the form that you send your line manager. We do not expect you to shoulder a financial burden for us. If you find that you are paying out of your own pocket more money than your personal finances can deal with, please get in contact with your line manager immediately and he/she will ensure that you are repaid immediately. When an expense is reimbursed, the Department of Taxation must be satisfied that the expense is allowable for tax purposes. If not, the repayment from an employer is treated as extra taxable income. Please consult your line manager or the finance department if you are not sure before you buy something you think will be a returnable expense. Tax law is continually changing, so again please consult the updated company guidelines available on the company intranet.

Travel

You can claim expenses for all your legitimate business travel, including when you travel to a temporary workplace. Examples of items you can claim for while on company business:

> Travel on planes, buses, ferries and taxis
> Parking, congestion charges, travel tolls
> Hotel bills and meals there
> Subsistence expenses (such as dining away from your usual workplace)
> An amount per kilometre using your own vehicle - this amount changes periodically
> $30 incidental expenses per day on day trips
> $60 incidental expenses per day on overnight trips

You cannot claim expenses for travel to and from your living place and usual office location.

Telephones and Internet

If you ever use your home phone or mobile for company business, you can claim the cost of these calls. You cannot claim the cost of rental or contract respectively, as this will be treated as a benefit in kind on which you will pay tax. If you use your own Internet connection, then you may only claim a proportion of the bill based on your company usage.

Entertainment

This can be a problematic area for the company when we make deductions against corporation tax. Expenses related to entertaining are allowed if they meet the following criteria:

> You are entertaining customers or potential customers
> None of your family or friends is present
> If the entertaining is not just a social event

You may be asked for details of any entertaining you claim for, so please try and acquire invoices for any items for which you plan to claim. The company can reimburse you for some expenses without proof of payment, but we try and keep this to a minimum.

SECTION 3   *Questions 28 – 40*

Read the following passage and answer Questions 28 – 40.

The Alvarez Hypothesis

In 1980, Luis and Walter Alvarez offered their meteorite impact theory after examining research sites around the world. Their hypothesis suggested that the mass extinction of the dinosaurs was caused by the impact of a large meteorite on Earth about sixty-five million years ago.

Meteorites are lumps of stony or metallic material that were parts of asteroids. Meteorites commonly collide with Earth, but the majority are destroyed in the impact with the Earth's atmosphere. Asteroids are planetary bodies or objects that revolve around the Sun and most are found in the asteroid belt between Mars and Jupiter. Some meteorites survive after entering the Earth's atmosphere and impact on the Earth's surface. The Alvarez Hypothesis theorises that a meteorite the size of San Francisco, travelling faster than a bullet, slammed into Earth sixty-five million years ago. The impact delivered a destructive blast thousands of times more powerful than the combined yield of all the world's nuclear weapons, setting off earthquakes greater than eleven in magnitude and widespread tsunamis, and shrouding the globe for years in a thick cocoon of sky-blackening dust and debris. This cataclysm effectively ended the reign of the dinosaurs and opened the door for the ascension of mammals.

The story began in 1977 in Gubbio, Italy, a tiny village halfway between Rome and Florence, where geologists Luis and Walter Alvarez were collecting samples of limestone rock for a paleomagnetism study. The limestone outside of Gubbio, which was once below the sea, provides total geological evidence of the end of the Cretaceous period and the beginning of the Tertiary period. This time span is sometimes referred to as "the Great Dying," because a massive extinction claimed nearly seventy-five per cent of all the species of life on our planet, including, in addition to the dinosaurs, most types of plants and many types of microscopic organisms. Luis and Walter Alvarez found that forming a distinct boundary between the limestone of the two periods was a thin layer of red clay. Immediately below this clay boundary, the Cretaceous limestone was heavily populated with a wide mix of the fossils of tiny marine creatures. Above the clay layer, in the Tertiary limestone, however, only the fossils of a single marine species could be seen. The clay layer itself contained no marine fossils at all.

The two geologists consulted two nuclear chemists in Berkley, who had developed a technique called neutron activation analysis. This enabled precise measurements of very low concentrations of elements. Luis Alvarez believed that neutron activation analysis would help determine how long it took for the clay layer to form. To the amazement of everyone involved, the measurements showed that the clay layer was about six hundred times richer in iridium than the surrounding limestone. Iridium, a silvery-white metallic element related to platinum, is virtually absent from the Earth's crust, but high concentrations are common in extraterrestrial objects, such as asteroids. These same iridium results were subsequently also discovered in clay layers at locations in Denmark and New Zealand, and later dozens of other sites around the world where the geological record of the Cretaceous-Tertiary boundaries is also complete. These iridium-spiked layers of clay also contained an abundance of soot.

The four scientists published their paper: "Extraterrestrial Cause for the Cretaceous-Tertiary Extinction". This paper was immediately resisted by scientific critics, who argued that volcanic eruptions were behind the demise of the dinosaurs and cited as evidence the thousands of miles of volcanic rock in an area of India known as the Deccan Traps. However, that argument was weakened by two subsequent findings. First, there was the discovery of shocked quartz along with the iridium and soot in the clay layer samples from around the world, which could only have been produced in the heat and violence of a titanic smash. Second came the discovery in 1991 of the scene of the titanic smash - the Chicxulub crater. This meteorite impact was thought to have caused the broken up quartz. The Chicxulub crater is a 180-kilometer-wide, 20-kilometer-deep impact crater off the northern coast of the Yucatan peninsula in the Gulf of Mexico that is buried a kilometre deep. The discovery of this impact site answered critics of the Alvarez Hypothesis who'd been demanding to know: if an asteroid impact killed the dinosaurs, where's the crater?

The Chicxulub crater was explored by drilling over two months. The crater nowadays is buried beneath a thousand meters of sediment. Under this is a layer of what is known as impact breccias and then a deposit of the impact melt. Beneath that is the rock that was needed to be brought to surface for research. The rock was shown to be made of anhydrite, which is a mineral that, if it were vaporised in an impact event, would produce the particular gases that could alter the Earth's weather.

The question of why the dinosaurs died out is still not definitively answered. Sixty-five million years ago is a large age gap to find conclusive evidence. Today, most scientists agree with the the Alvarez Hypothesis and that the Earth was indeed struck by a large meteorite at the end of the Cretaceous period. Whether this was the actual reason the dinosaurs died out or whether it was only a contributing factor will probably never be proved.

Questions 28 – 34

Choose the correct letter **A, B, C or D**.

Write the correct letter in boxes **28 - 34** on your answer sheet.

28   Most meteorites colliding with Earth
    A   usually have trajectories that head towards the sun.
    B   are broken up when they enter the Earth's atmosphere.
    C   are usually found beyond the farthest planet.
    D   lost their power to threaten Earth millions of years ago.

29   The Alvarez Hypothesis theorised that the impact of the meteorite
   A   triggered a nuclear explosion.
   B   was preceded by a series of earthquakes.
   C   had no effect on sea life.
   D   darkened the sky of the Earth.

30   Gubbio was a good place to research for Luis and Walter Alvarez, because
   A   it was close to where they lived.
   B   the area had a strong magnetic field.
   C   rock there provides a complete geological record of the relevant time frame.
   D   it is close to the sea.

31   "The Great Dying" was a time when
   A   all life on Earth was wiped out.
   B   almost three-quarters of life on Earth was wiped out.
   C   only plants were left alive on Earth.
   D   only a few dinosaurs were left alive.

32   The thin layer of red clay found by Luis and Walter Alvarez
   A   was coloured by the decay of the limestone on either side.
   B   had no fossils from the sea.
   C   contained only a few dinosaur fossils.
   D   was a record of the first few million years of the Tertiary period.

33   The surprise from the neutron activation analysis results was
   A   how exact the measurements were.
   B   how fast the clay layer took to form.
   C   how slow the clay layer took to form.
   D   how high the levels of a certain element were.

34   Samples around the world from the same time period also showed
   A   uneven results of iridium.
   B   the Cretaceous period ended at different times around the world.
   C   high levels of soot.
   D   similar fossil records.

Questions 35 – 37

*Complete each sentence with the correct ending (**A** - **F**) below.*

*Write the correct letter (**A** - **F**) in answer boxes **35** - **37** on your answer sheet.*

35   The paper that was published on the Alvarez Hypothesis

36   The impact of the meteorite 65 million years ago

37   The site of the Chicxulub crater

A   was not published until some time later.

B   was discovered after the initial publication of the Alvarez Hypothesis.

C   was initially preferred to the theory of volcanic eruptions killing the dinosaurs.

D   was not accepted at once by fellow scientists.

E   was replaced by soot in some research sites around the world.

F   was later thought to be responsible for the broken up quartz in the rock samples.

Questions 38 – 40

Label the diagram below.

Write **NO MORE THAN TWO WORDS** from the text for each answer.

Write your answers in boxes **38 - 40** on your answer sheet.

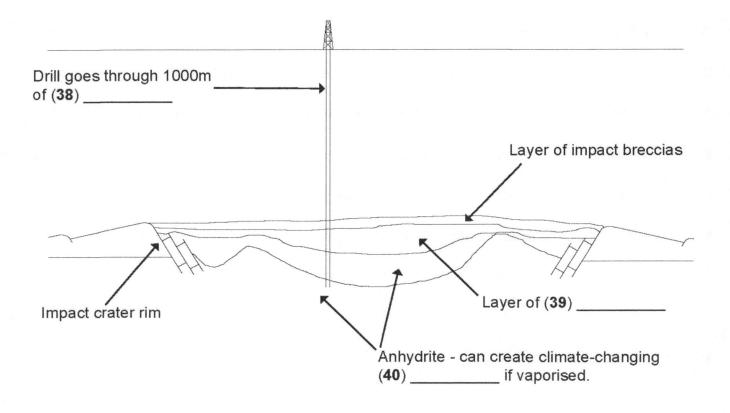

**Drilling Operations at
the Chicxlub Crater**

Drill goes through 1000m
of (**38**) _____

Layer of impact breccias

Impact crater rim

Layer of (**39**) _____

Anhydrite - can create climate-changing
(**40**) _____ if vaporised.

WRITING

WRITING TASK 1

You should spend about 20 minutes on this task.

You and your neighbours have noticed that the rubbish collection services where you live have recently been quite bad.

Write a letter to your local council. In your letter,

- **explain what you have recently experienced**
- **explain what the neighbours have recently experienced**
- **ask what action will be taken to improve the service**

You should write at least 150 words.

*You do **NOT** need to write any addresses. Begin your letter as follows:*

Dear Sir / Madam,

WRITING TASK 2

You should spend about 40 minutes on this task.

Write about the following topic:

Today's society provides people with various ways to lose weight, such as special diets or exercise regimes. Many people believe though that poor food and today's lifestyle should be addressed first.

What is your viewpoint of this situation?

Give reasons for your answer and include any relevant examples from your knowledge or experience.

You should write at least 250 words.

SPEAKING

PART 1

- Can you describe one of the rooms in your house/flat?
- Do you prefer living in a big house/flat or a small one? (Why?)
- What are some of the disadvantages of living in a big house?

Topic 1   Entertainment
- What is the most popular form of entertainment in your country?
- Do people in your country usually prefer to go out or stay at home in the evenings?
- Why do you think that successful entertainers are often paid so much?
- How popular is watching sport in your country as a form of entertainment?

Topic 2   Teenagers
- What is life like for a teenager in your country?
- What are some of the challenges that teenagers face today?
- Do you think teenagers should be allowed to drive? (Why/Why not?)
- What are parents' attitudes to boyfriends and girlfriends for teenagers in your country?

PART 2

Describe something you have bought recently
You should say:
        what it is
        where you bought it
        what it looks like
and explain why you needed to buy this thing.

PART 3

Topic 1   Luxury
- What luxury item would you choose if you could have any one thing?
- Do you think luxury possessions bring happiness? (Why/Why not?)
- Should luxury items be taxed at a higher rate? (Why/Why not?)
- How have the lives of rich people changed over the last 30 years?

Topic 2   The Food Supply
- Where is your country's food mainly produced?
- What are some of the challenges that face food producers today?
- Do you believe that the world should use genetically modified food? (Why/Why not?)
- How can we reduce the amount of food wasted today both domestically and commercially?

PRACTICE TEST 5

Download audio recordings for the test here:
https://www.ielts-blog.com/ielts-practice-tests-downloads/
Need help with audio content? Contact the author via
email simone@ielts-blog.com and expect a quick response.

LISTENING

PART 1   *Questions 1 – 10*

Questions 1 – 5

Complete Roger's customer form below.

*Write **NO MORE THAN THREE WORDS AND/OR A NUMBER** from the listening for each answer.*

Southern Trains
Special Ticket Form

Type of Ticket:	Season
Customer's Name:	Sandra (**1**) _____
Address:	(**2**) _____ Andover Way Stanton ST6 3ED
Date of Birth:	8th October (**3**) _____
Previous Ticket:	YES / (NO)
Email Address:	sandra@(**4**) _____.com
Telephone: Home: Work: Cell:	n/a n/a 05 (**5**) _____ 495 712

Questions 6 – 10

*Circle the correct letters **A** - **C**.*

6   For what journey will Sandra use her season ticket?

    A   Stanton to Bexington
    B   Stanton to Petersfield
    C   Stanton to Amberton

7   What type of ticket options does Sandra choose?

    A   Off-peak with weekends
    B   Peak with weekends
    C   Peak without weekends

8   What class of season ticket does Sandra choose?

    A   First class
    B   Second class
    C   Variable class

9   What is the monthly price of Sandra's season ticket?

    A $98
    B $158.40
    C $172

10   From which platform will Sandra's trains leave?

    A   4
    B   7
    C   6

PART 2   Questions 11 - 20

Questions 11 – 15

*Match the correct level at the Paradise Hotel with the needs given in questions **11 - 15**.*

Level 1   Level 2   Level 3   Level 4
Level 5   Level 6   Level 7

11   A guest wants to see the concierge.

12   A guest wants to go to room 412.

13   A guest wants to go to the beach.

14   A guest wants to eat at the seafood restaurant.

15   A guest wants to do a yoga class.

Questions 16 – 20

*Answer the questions below. Write **NO MORE THAN THREE WORDS AND/OR A NUMBER** from the listening for each answer.*

16   When will Monday's entertainment evening end?

17   Where will the quiz be held?

18   Who will sing the first song at the karaoke night?

19   Where can people book a table for the jazz night?

20   Where will live music be playing on Saturday and Sunday evenings?

PART 3   Questions 21 – 30

Questions 21 and 22

Complete the table below on the advantages and disadvantages of the cigarette factory site.

*Write **NO MORE THAN TWO WORDS** from the listening for each answer.*

Location	Advantages	Disadvantages
Cigarette factory in town centre	Convenient Possible grants from the (**21**) _____	No room for a (**22**) _____ High site cost

Questions 23 – 25

Complete the sentences below.

*Write **NO MORE THAN TWO WORDS** from the listening for each answer.*

23   The financial part of the students' project includes detailing start-up costs and ten years of _____ of revenue.

24   Tony points out that lots of construction work for _____ would be required to shelter the field survey site from flooding.

25   Because there is always a lot of people travelling to the airport, there is lots of _____ already in place.

Questions 26 – 29

Who will do each of the following jobs?

A	Alison
B	Tony
C	Sophie
D	Greg

*Write the correct letter, **A, B, C or D** on your answer sheet.*

26   Obtain permission to be on the land they want to survey

27   Search for other development plans on the land they want to survey

28   Text the postcode of the land they want to survey

29   Check that the equipment is free

Question 30

*Choose the correct letter **A, B, or C**.*

30   How did Tony get the money with which he will pay the deposit?

   A   A bank loan
   B   Some work he did
   C   Borrowed it from his parents

PART 4   Questions 31 – 40

Questions 31 – 34

Complete the table below on events related to tea mentioned in the listening.

Write **NO MORE THAN TWO WORDS** from the listening for each answer.

Time Frame	Events
200 B.C.	First records of tea drunk in (**31**) _____
Latter ½ of the 16th century	Tea mentioned as a drink for Europeans
Last years of the 16th century	Dutch import tea to Europe commercially as they take over Portuguese (**32**) _____
The seventeenth century	British adopted tea
1689	First (**33**) _____ on tea in leaf form
The eighteenth century	Debate over whether tea is healthy or not
The mid - nineteenth century	Temperance movement recommended tea as an alternative to (**34**) _____
1964	Tax on tea is abolished

Questions 35 – 37

Label the pie chart below on world tea consumption. Write **NO MORE THAN THREE WORDS AND/OR A NUMBER** from the listening for each answer.

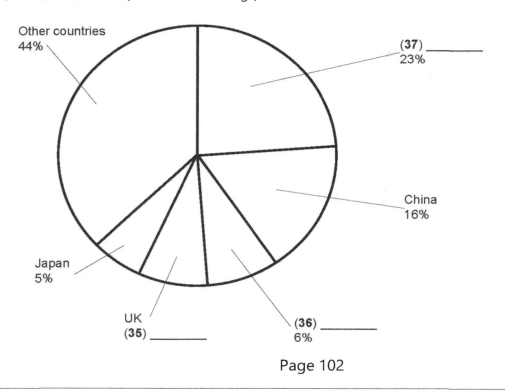

Questions 38 – 40

Complete the flow chart describing the process for making tea below. Write **NO MORE THAN ONE WORD AND/OR A NUMBER** from the listening for each answer.

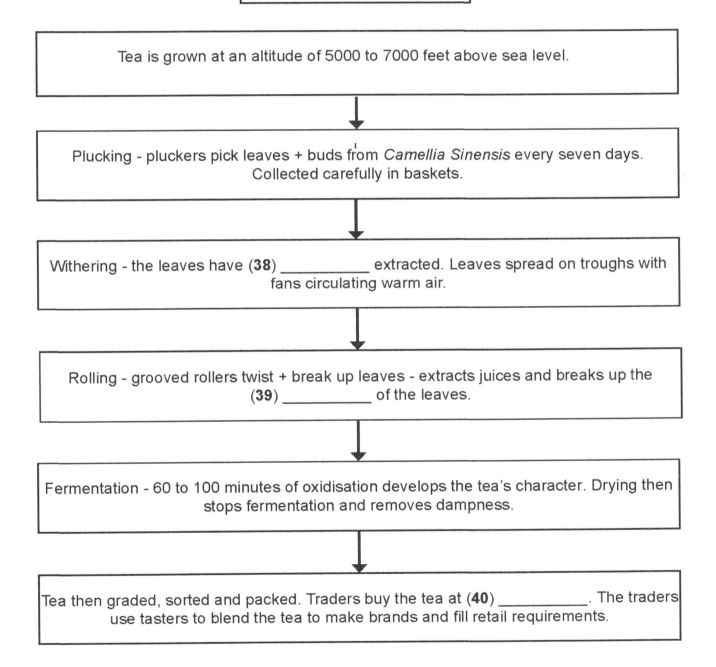

The Process for Making Tea

Tea is grown at an altitude of 5000 to 7000 feet above sea level.

↓

Plucking - pluckers pick leaves + buds from *Camellia Sinensis* every seven days. Collected carefully in baskets.

↓

Withering - the leaves have (**38**) _____ extracted. Leaves spread on troughs with fans circulating warm air.

↓

Rolling - grooved rollers twist + break up leaves - extracts juices and breaks up the (**39**) _____ of the leaves.

↓

Fermentation - 60 to 100 minutes of oxidisation develops the tea's character. Drying then stops fermentation and removes dampness.

↓

Tea then graded, sorted and packed. Traders buy the tea at (**40**) _____. The traders use tasters to blend the tea to make brands and fill retail requirements.

READING

SECTION 1   *Questions 1 – 14*

Questions 1 – 7

*There are six advertisements on the next page, **A - F**.*

Which advertisement mentions the following information?

*Write the correct letter, **A - F**, in boxes **1 – 7** on your answer sheet.*

1   This advertisement is for a service that is not carried out in people's homes.

2   This advertisement is for a service that can look after children.

3   This advertisement is for a service that can take place the day people call.

4   This advertisement is for a service that can help prevent a potentially dangerous situation.

5   This advertisement is for a service that has its work covered by insurance.

6   This advertisement is for a service that can supply recommendations from previously satisfied customers.

7   This advertisement is for a service that can be contacted by email.

A   Greenstar Drain Solutions

We: unblock drains, toilets, sinks, urinals, pipes, manholes...

Prompt and reliable 24-hour service - no call-out charge

Call your local drain engineer on 01863 854 932

www.greenstardrains.com

B   Repair and Service

Don't want to spend lots of money with branded servicing of your home appliances?

We will visit you to repair and service all makes of:

washing machines	cookers
dishwashers	tumble driers
fridge freezers	ovens

Same day service available.

www.magnatraining.com

C   Handy Andy - *your local handyman*
Come to us for all your home odd job needs.

- Free estimates
- Carpentry a speciality
- Painting and decorating
- Gardening and landscaping
- Roofing
- Member of your local tradesmen's association
- Fully insured

Call Andy on 01462 859 823
or contact him on handyandy@living.com

D   David English - MOT Testing

Every day, many satisfied customers leave our premises with their cars having passed their MOT car safety check. We have the experience and dedication to ensure that your car will sail through its check. We carry a wide selection of parts that often cause MOT failure, so you won't be left waiting for your vehicle. Drop your car off with us today or call us for more information on:

01462 975 883

No work is ever carried out before consultation with the owner!

E   Alice Stoneman
your local cleaner

Call me to make an appointment for me to clean your home. I can also iron, launder, cook and babysit.

All at highly competitive rates!

For your peace of mind, I have an up-to-date "police-checked" certificate.
AND
I can supply lots of genuine references with telephone numbers for you to double-check.

Call me, Alice, on 07770 888 231.

F   Chimney Cleaning - **Tom Johnson** - 01462 863 054

In today's gas and electricity-powered world, coming across a real fire at home is getting more and more difficult. Even more difficult is locating someone with expertise and experience to perform the essential annual cleaning of the chimney and hearth. A badly maintained chimney can cause excessive dirt and a risk of fire. Call me, Tom, today to arrange a visit and a quote.

Questions 8 – 14

Do the following statements agree with the information given in the text?

*In boxes **8 – 14** on your answer sheet write:*

TRUE	*if the statement agrees with the information*
FALSE	*if the statement contradicts the information*
NOT GIVEN	*if there is no information on this*

8   The library is closed for maintenance once a month on the first Monday of each month.

9   If you become a member online, you can pick up your membership card the same day.

10   Under 16's and old age pensioners have reduced rates when borrowing audiobooks, music CD's and DVD's.

11   You can borrow a book for at least five weeks if you renew it.

12   Using the Inter Library Loan service incurs a small fee.

13   Library computer reservations cannot be made by email.

14   Babies at the singing sessions can learn to interact better with their peers.

Illington Public library

Opening Hours

Monday 10 a.m. - 5 p.m.	Friday 9.30 a.m. - 7 p.m.
Tuesday 9.30 a.m. - 7 p.m.	Saturday 9.30 a.m. - 1 p.m.
Wednesday Closed	*Sunday Closed*
Thursday 9.30 a.m. - 7 p.m.	

Joining the Library   Membership of the library services is free. You can join without delay at the library when you come to visit us by presenting proof of your name and current address. You can join also online and then pick up your library card one day later when you visit us and show us your ID.

Borrowing

You will be able to borrow:

- 10 books or audiobooks for 4 weeks
- 8 music CD's for 2 weeks
- 5 DVD's for 2 weeks

You will usually have to pay to borrow audiobooks, music CD's, and DVD's. Please ask staff about concessions and special offers. If the item you require isn't available, you may reserve it online or at any library.

Renewals - You can renew items for a further 2 weeks (up to a maximum of 3 times) in person, by telephone, or online. If you telephone, please have your library card and the items to hand.

Inter Library Loans   If you want a book or journal article that the library does not hold, you can request it free of charge through Inter Library Loans. The inter-lending team will try to obtain a copy from another Library Authority, but you must be a member of the Library.

Library Computers   We have 10 computers which can be booked by members of the public in the library. Booking can only be done in person or by telephone. From the library computers, you can access the Internet, including web based e-mail. Computers also have word processing and desktop publishing software installed. You can print items if you wish, at a small extra cost per sheet. In the children's section, there are 5 separate computers for use only by children under 14.

Events for Babies   Every week, we hold a singing session for babies and toddlers and their mothers. Everyone sits in a circle with the children and we all sing songs with them. These songs can be modern favourites or traditional nursery rhymes. The facilitator brings with him / her musical instruments, which are used for some songs. Singing the songs with your baby in this environment can help with their speech development, sense of timing, confidence and social skills.

Children's Reading Group   For older children (4 – 8), we organise times when the library staff will be on hand to help children choose books and take them out. There are also reading sessions when children can listen to a member of staff reading a selected book. See the website for details for which books are being read and when.

SECTION 2   *Questions 15 – 27*

Questions 15 – 21

Complete the sentences below.

*Write **NO MORE THAN TWO WORDS** from the text for each answer.*

*Write your answers in boxes **15 - 21** on your answer sheet.*

15   People often fear starting a website for their business because of the costs and their own lack of _____.

16   Constructing a website with E-Serve always begins with a fact-finding _____.

17   E-Serve can set up online operations for start-up businesses or _____.

18   Customers won't receive _____ as the pricing of hosting with E-Serve is transparent.

19   One of E-Serve's _____ can explain to potential customers what is needed in terms of e-Marketing.

20   Websites often need to be altered, due to the extremely _____ nature of business today.

21   The best levels of written _____ are essential for a secure website.

E-Serve - The Best Website Hosting in Town

Having a website for a business today is a must, though some people shy away from it because they fear the expense and feel they are short of the technical knowledge. Here at E-Serve, we offer an affordable service and take care of all the specialised aspects, so you can focus on your business and products or services.

Making a Website   We create everything you need for a professional website. We will start with a consultation with you to find out what you require. We will then create a mock-up, so you can see what things will look like before we carry on. After that, we will make your website, while constantly in contact with you, so that things end up the way you want them.

e-Commerce   Not every business operates their selling online, but if you want this option, we have lots of experience with setting up a system that will suit you. We can cover all types of business, from beginners to worldwide traders. Changing your package is easy, and we can help your systems change and grow as your business does. Being safe is an essential part of any transaction that takes place over the Internet. Customer will lose his/her faith in your e-business if he/she fears it is not safe. Our e-Commerce is state-of-the-art and the security protocols are unrivalled.

Hosting   With so many offers on the market, it can be hard to make a choice. We have various transparent packages that you can choose from. We never lock you into a contract, so you can withdraw at any time or change your package without incurring any unexpected charges. We only use the very latest hardware from the world's leading manufacturers to deliver optimum performance and super-fast page loading times for your website.

e-Marketing   Having a website is not just about sticking a website onto the Web and waiting for the business to come to you. Operating a website on the Internet nowadays means marketing it hard through all aspects of social media, online PR and what is known as search engine optimisation. We can train you in all this or do a lot of it for you. It's a complex business, so contact one of our sales executives who can give details on what you need to know and how exactly we can help you.

Client Training   Nowadays, businesses are tremendously dynamic and we understand that you will want to change your website from time to time. To save you having to ask us to change your website, we will train you to operate our systems, so that you can make the changes cheaply and when you want them. You won't need any knowledge of web design, coding or computer languages. You will just need to log into our client interface and use our custom-made operating system to make your changes. Training will take place when your website is complete and refresher courses can be taken throughout the year. The training and refresher courses are all free of charge.

Security   Web sites are unfortunately prone to security risks. For your business to succeed, clients need to trust that they have protection from viruses, hackers and identity thieves. Your relative security is high if you have few network resources of financial value, your company and site aren't controversial in any way, your network is set up with tight permissions, your web server is patched up to date with all settings done correctly, your applications on the web server are all patched and updated, and your website code is done to high standards. You can count on our site set up to keep your website secure, your visitors safe and your business growing.

Questions 22 – 27

Answer the questions below.

Write **NO MORE THAN THREE WORDS AND/OR A NUMBER** from the text for each answer.

Write your answers in boxes **22 - 27** on your answer sheet.

22   From when do employees begin to build up paid sick leave?

23   Who should employees telephone if they are too sick to come to work?

24   When will employees have to make up work if they call in sick at the weekend?

25   What must employees have acquired during sickness if the company is to put changes into place?

26   After how long can a company terminate the employment of someone on long-term sickness?

27   What organisation can be appealed to if employees feel they have been fired without cause?

Calling in Sick

Everyone gets sick once in a while and we've issued these guidelines, so that you as an employee know what to do when this happens.

All our staff accrue paid sick leave (PSL) from their first day. You will be able to use your accrued PSL as paid time off...

- ... to deal with our own illness, injury or health condition.
- ... to take care of a family member (including domestic partners) with an illness, injury or medical appointment.

You only need a sick note from a doctor after three days in a row of being sick (including weekends). If you are ill just before or during your holiday, you can take it as sick leave instead.

When you realise that you feel too ill to come to work, you should please call the absence manager as soon as you can. When talking to him/her, briefly explain what you think is wrong with you and, if possible, when you might come back to work. If you can't get through to your line manager, write an email as soon as you can. It's important that we know you're sick as early as possible, so we can arrange cover for you to cope with urgent business that you would normally deal with.

As our company operates at weekends, we have a policy that states that if you call in sick at the weekend, you have to come in the following weekend. This is not to punish you, but only to cover the time of the worker who has to work to cover you.

We understand that a lot of people feel some guilt about calling in sick. However, the health of our workforce is a priority for us. Sick workers do not perform well and make mistakes and often they can pass on their illnesses to their colleagues. So, unless it's very necessary for you, don't work. If you are sick, you need to focus on getting better. Don't spend your day still working and checking emails. You should focus on getting well so that you can make it back into the workplace as soon as you can.

If you have developed disabilities during your sickness, we are obliged to make reasonable adjustments to your work conditions, which could include shorter hours or adapting equipment.

If you are off work sick for more than four weeks, you will be considered long-term sick. A long-term sick employee is still entitled to annual leave. After eight months, we can dismiss an employee who is long-term sick, but before we can do this, we must:

- consider if you can return to work – e.g. working flexibly or part-time, doing different or less stressful work (with training if necessary).
- consult with you about when you could return to work and if your health will improve.

You can take your case to an employment tribunal if you think you've been unfairly dismissed. If you've been off work for longer than one month for whatever reason, you'll be required to attend a 'return to work interview'. This will be informal and brief and include questions like 'how do you feel about being back at work?' We want to welcome an employee back and check that they are well enough to be working, find out why they were away and let them know any news.

SECTION 3   *Questions 28 - 40*

*Read the following text and answer Questions **28 – 40**.*

Corks have been used as bottle stoppers for as long as we have had wine. The Greeks in the fifth century BCE sometimes used corks to close wine jugs. Following in their footsteps, the Romans also used the cork as a stopper and also coated corks with pitch to seal the closure. Cork was not immediately as successful as it is today and historian, Sally Marshall, explains why. "Cork's success as a closure depends upon its fitting snugly into an opening with a relatively uniform diameter. Thus, it was not until the seventeenth century, when glass bottles were first made with openings more or less the same size, that the cork truly came into its own."

Every time someone buys a bottle sealed with a natural cork stopper, they are helping to sustain one of the world's most biodiverse forests and protect an extraordinary ecosystem and industry. Using cork also helps protecting jobs. Jose Rivera, a Portuguese cork grower, explains. "While it might seem counterintuitive, the best way to ensure that there is no shortage of cork is to use more cork. That is because the greater the demand for cork, the greater the economic incentive there will be to protect the cork oak forests for future generations."

Cork's unique attributes make it a multipurpose material. Because cork is composed of a honeycomb of microscopic cells, it is very light, easy to compress yet strong, impermeable to liquids and gases, adaptable to temperature and pressure, an insulator against moisture and noise, and resistant to fire. When it comes to preserving wine, cork allows just the right amount of oxygen to interact with the liquid, making it the perfect material to allow wine to age properly. Wine connoisseur, Jean Costaud, says it also adds to the wine experience. "It's all to do with when the wine is opened. No artificial stopper can come close to reproducing the iconic "pop" when the cork is removed."

With all the beneficial properties of corks as bottle closures, there is one significant defect. This is "corkiness", a condition that exists when wine is tainted by the presence of a chemical compound called 2, 4, 6 - Trichloroanisole - TCA for short. This compound appears to be caused in the cork by the interaction of moisture, chlorine and mould that is always there. Corks are exposed to these elements during their production and TCA can form. Unfortunately, the human nose can detect this "corkiness" at concentrations as low as four parts per trillion! Jean Costaud explains the problem. "A lightly corked wine may simply smell like cork, while a badly corked wine smells musty, like damp cardboard or old newspapers. The usual rich aroma and taste of the wine is stripped away by the musty odor."

Artificial corks and screw tops are the two main alternatives to natural wood corks. An artificial cork is made of ethylene vinyl acetate. It looks and feels very similar to real cork and a corkscrew is used to remove it from the bottle. It has two drawbacks: one is that it often fits so tightly in the bottle that it is very difficult to remove (a problem that will no doubt be resolved through research). American wine producer, Alice Deacon, is more interested in the second, more technical problem. "We want to know whether the synthetic material is truly non-reactive and inert over long periods of time. Will it impart any tastes of its own to the wine?" Naturally, wineries using these plastic corks are deliberately aging wines to see what happens, but it is too soon by several years to know the outcome. Nonetheless, more and more low- and mid-range producers are switching to an artificial cork.

The screw cap provides an excellent air-tight seal, although there is a question as to whether or not it will protect the wine over a very long period of time. The problem with the screw cap is psychological. Wine merchant, Mary Winters sums up her clients' feelings. "The image of a screw cap is firmly lodged in many minds as the epitome of cheap wine. Because of this, many of the fine wine producers we deal with are sensitive to the fine wine market. They hesitate to switch to a screw cap, because they do not want their wine to be perceived as of inferior quality."

Supporters of cork publicise its environmentally-friendly properties. The 6.6 million acres of cork oak forests in the Mediterranean Basin not only serve as a refuge for endangered species, they also help reduce greenhouse emissions. Environmentalist, Charles Wrathe, explains. "It seems like a small thing, but every cork stopper represents a carbon offset of 113.5 grams. Looked at differently, the 6.6 million acres of Mediterranean cork oaks capture approximately 14.4 million metric tons of carbon dioxide."

While waiting for the wine industry to make up its mind, cork has diversified. In recent years, fashion designers and shoe manufacturers have started to use cork to create their signature footwear. Mike Baker, a CEO at a footwear company, is a big fan. "The transformation of used wine corks into durable and attractive footwear is an easy and elegant way to extend the life-cycle of this remarkable material while providing consumers with a terrific and fashionable new product that literally lightens their carbon footprint." Another use for cork has been the development of a floor tile manufactured from cork. Sally Marshall explains the advantages. "Amazingly, cork floor tiles are a great product. They are lightweight, permeable, physically resilient and chemically inert. They provide excellent insulation due to their low thermal conductivity and have a high compressive strength." First made in the US in 1899, they were made originally by fusing together cork shavings using asphalt. Nowadays, a combination of intense heat and pressure enables cork shavings to be fused together without a glue or binder and phenolic resin and urea resins are added to strengthen the tiles. Cork floor tiling is a really beautiful eco product with only one drawback: excessive moisture can result in absorption and deterioration of the binder, causing the cork composition to loosen and eventually buckle.

Questions 28 – 35

*Look at the following statements (questions **28 - 35**) and the list of people below.*

Match each statement with the correct person's initials.

*Write the correct initials in boxes **28 - 35** on your answer sheet.*

28   Screw caps can create the perception of a lower class product.

29   Real corks even have a satisfying auditory effect on the person opening a bottle.

30   There is a worry that artificial corks may also affect a wine's flavour.

31   Cork only became widely used when manufacturing methods were able to create uniformly-sized bottles.

32   Used real corks can be recycled as shoes.

33   Real corks can sometimes negatively affect the flavour of the wine.

34   Even a single real cork can help protect the environment.

35   Using as much real cork as possible will ensure there is no shortage of the material.

SM	Sally Marshall
JR	Jose Rivera
JC	Jean Costaud
AD	Alice Deacon
MW	Mary Winters
CW	Charles Wrathe
MB	Mike Baker

Questions 36 – 39

Choose **FOUR** letters, **A - H**.

Which of the following sentences below accurately describe information regarding cork given in the text?

Write the correct letter, **A - H**, in any order in boxes **36 - 39** on your answer sheet.

A   Cork does not allow any air at all to reach a bottle's contents.

B   There is moisture in a cork that can lead to a wine bottle's contents being spoiled.

C   Artificial corks closely resemble real corks.

D   Wine producers have sent their product to university laboratories to assess the long-term effect of artificial corks.

E   Artificial cork use is becoming more popular with wine producers.

F   Cork is no longer grown around the Mediterranean.

G   Treated cork does not react with other compounds.

H   Cork is a difficult material to recycle.

Question 40

Choose the correct letter, **A, B, C or D**.

Write the correct letter in box **40** on your answer sheet.

40   What is the best title for the text in section 3?

     A   A Material for the Future
     B   Cork: A Versatile Material
     C   The End of the Line for Cork
     D   How Cork is Manufactured

WRITING

WRITING TASK 1

You should spend about 20 minutes on this task.

> **You have decided to go on a holiday to a foreign country for 2 weeks, and you want one of your friends to go with you.**
>
> **Write a letter to your friend asking him to accompany you. In your letter,**
>
> - **explain where and when you want to go**
> - **give details of the travel, dates and costs involved**
> - **describe some of the things you want to do**

You should write at least 150 words.

*You do **NOT** need to write any addresses. Begin your letter as follows:*

> ***Dear John,***

WRITING TASK 2

You should spend about 40 minutes on this task.

Write about the following topic:

> **Many people nowadays travel abroad for their university education.**
>
> **Why do people do this and would / will you consider doing this yourself?**

Give reasons for your answer and include any relevant examples from your knowledge or experience.

You should write at least 250 words.

SPEAKING

PART 1

- Can you tell me about a shop that is near where you live?
- Who does the shopping in your household?
- Do you prefer shopping in smaller family-owned shops or larger supermarkets? (Why?)

Topic 1   Newspapers and the News
- Do you like to read newspapers? (Why/Why not?)
- Why do people like to be kept up-to-date with the news?
- With the rise of the Internet, do you think paper newspapers will soon be a thing of the past? (Why/Why not?)
- Why is there always a focus on bad news?

Topic 2   Languages
- What languages can you speak?
- Do you think people at school should study a foreign language? (Why/Why not?)
- What are some of the advantages of speaking various languages well?
- Do you think English will keep its importance in the years to come?

PART 2

Describe a memorable party that you went to.
You should say:
          whose party it was
          when the party was
          who was at the party
and explain why this party was so memorable.

PART 3

Topic 1   Celebrations
- What events in your country are celebrated by holding a party?
- What is a polite way of refusing a party invitation?
- What kinds of decisions and considerations are needed when planning a party?
- What are the characteristics of a good host and hostess at a party?

Topic 2   Parties and Alcohol
- What is your viewpoint about people drinking alcohol at a party?
- How should the police deal with people who get out of control at parties because of alcohol?
- How do you think attitudes to alcohol have changed in your country over the last 30 years?
- What can be done to stop young people abusing alcohol?

Listening Test Answer Sheet

1		21	
2		22	
3		23	
4		24	
5		25	
6		26	
7		27	
8		28	
9		29	
10		30	
11		31	
12		32	
13		33	
14		34	
15		35	
16		36	
17		37	
18		38	
19		39	
20		40	

Reading Test Answer Sheet

1		21	
2		22	
3		23	
4		24	
5		25	
6		26	
7		27	
8		28	
9		29	
10		30	
11		31	
12		32	
13		33	
14		34	
15		35	
16		36	
17		37	
18		38	
19		39	
20		40	

Answers

LISTENING ANSWERS

/ indicates an alternative answer   ( ) indicates an optional answer

TEST 1	TEST 2	TEST 3	TEST 4	TEST 5
1. Simpson	1. May	1. 1982	1. Easton	1. Williams
2. 13	2. Truman	2. 30	2. 30	2. 43
3. 7RT	3. 6 p.m.	3. Wright	3. October	3. 1994
4. 7.30	4. Horse riding	4. 981	4. hotels.com	4. primrose
5. F23	5. 30	5. Direct debit	5. Commission	5. 482
6. B*	6. 7	6. 2 gigabytes/GB	6. 13	6. A
7. C*	7. 6	7. SIM (card)	7. sea view	7. C
8. E*	8. 5	8. 30	8. 2,000	8. C
9. G*	9. 400	9. 45	9. deposit	9. B
10. K*	10. 100	10. link	10. Breakfast	10. B
11. J	11. L	11. A*	11. 1924	11. Level 3
12. F	12. S	12. E*	12. 25	12. Level 4
13. B	13. F	13. H*	13. (health and) safety	13. Level 7
14. E	14. R	14. K*	14. ingredients	14. Level 2
15. C	15. A	15. O*	15. Wrapping	15. Level 1
16. Some fruit	16. C	16. residents	16. lecture	16. 10 (p.m.)
17. The 2nd floor	17. C*	17. 5-minute	17. guide	17. The rooftop bar
18. 1	18. D*	18. 4	18. 10	18. The hotel manager
19. On the terrace	19. F*	19. (warming-up) exercises	19. 13	19. At the reception
20. In the restaurant	20. G*	20. (bus) driver	20. wheelchair	20. By the pool
21. 50%	21. farmers	21. C	21. periods	21. (town) council
22. cliff formations	22. field	22. C	22. specialisation	22. car park
23. global warming	23. growth	23. B	23. essays	23. forecasts
24. hotspots / hot spots	24. acidity	24. A	24. reading	24. protection
25. overnight	25. season	25. B	25. projects	25. road access
26. consequences	26. hard copy	26. land owner	26. B*	26. A
27. foreign students	27. 30th April	27. (family) group/family	27. D*	27. D
28. 2 hours	28. 2000	28. rangers	28. F*	28. B
29. exam	29. appendices	29. (big) paths	29. C	29. A
30. course tutors	30. graduate	30. secret	30. B	30. B
31. fat	31. A	31. 10,000	31. natural dip	31. China
32. killer whales	32. C	32. equipment	32. clay	32. trading routes
33. C	33. C	33. by-catch	33. The saturation level	33. tax
34. A	34. B	34. (commercial) (fishing) companies	34. A (natural) spring	34. alcohol
35. B	35. A	35. B	35. ecosystems	35. 6%
36. overfishing	36. (personality) characteristics	36. A	36. urbanisation	36. Russia
37. 2 degrees	37. variance	37. C	37. evaporates	37. India
38. nesting areas	38. guidance	38. 91	38. tap (system)	38. moisture
39. breeding platforms	39. shorthand	39. ecosystems	39. tanks	39. cells
40. food	40. nervous	40. economies	40. balance of payments	40. auctions
Note: Answers for qu. 6, 7, 8, 9 and 10 can be written in any order	**Note:** Answers for qu. 17, 18, 19 and 20 can be written in any order	**Note:** Answers for qu. 11, 12, 13, 14 and 15 can be written in any order	**Note:** Answers for qu. 26, 27, and 28 can be written in any order	

READING ANSWERS

/ indicates an alternative answer   ( ) indicates an optional answer

TEST 1	TEST 2	TEST 3	TEST 4	TEST 5
1. B	1. E	1. D	1. hoses	1. D
2. A	2. D	2. E	2. transit bars	2. E
3. C	3. C	3. B	3. ventilation	3. B
4. F	4. A	4. F	4. flooding	4. F
5. E	5. C	5. C	5. detergent	5. C
6. A	6. C	6. E	6. energy consumption	6. E
7. C	7. B	7. A	7. landfill sites	7. C
8. TRUE	8. E	8. F	8. plastic	8. NOT GIVEN
9. TRUE	9. F	9. D	9. on the pavement	9. FALSE
10. NOT GIVEN	10. B	10. status	10. building waste	10. NOT GIVEN
11. FALSE	11. D	11. driver	11. using prepaid cards	11. TRUE
12. FALSE	12. C	12. photo	12. FALSE	12. FALSE
13. NOT GIVEN	13. G	13. register	13. TRUE	13. TRUE
14. TRUE	14. H	14. insurance	14. NOT GIVEN	14. TRUE
15. time management skills	15. line manager	15. TRUE	15. liabilities	15. (technical) knowledge
16. dialogue	16. company website	16. FALSE	16. same legal entity	16. consultation
17. products	17. email address	17. TRUE	17. insolvent	17. worldwide traders
18. goals	18. complaints meeting	18. NOT GIVEN	18. partnership agreement	18. unexpected charges
19. complainer	19. mediator	19. FALSE	19. taxation	19. sales executives
20. competitive	20. written record	20. NOT GIVEN	20. provisions	20. dynamic
21. smile	21. footrest	21. TRUE	21. FALSE	21. website code
22. NO	22. cross	22. D	22. TRUE	22. Their first day
23. NO	23. stand	23. B	23. TRUE	23. The absence manager
24. NOT GIVEN	24. extended periods	24. G	24. NOT GIVEN	24. The following weekend
25. YES	25. keyboard	25. A	25. TRUE	25. disabilities
26. YES	26. glare	26. F	26. NOT GIVEN	26. 8 months
27. NOT GIVEN	27. bifocals	27. H	27. FALSE	27. An employment tribunal
28. I	28. E	28. ii	28. B	28. MW
29. B	29. B	29. i	29. D	29. JC
30. E	30. A	30. viii	30. C	30. AD
31. D	31. D	31. vi	31. B	31. SM
32. K	32. C	32. v	32. B	32. MB
33. J	33. B	33. x	33. D	33. JC
34. France	34. D	34. vii	34. C	34. CW
35. In the fridge	35. B	35. iii	35. D	35. JR
36. The cosmetics brands	36. E	36. YES	36. F	36. B*
37. 3-roll mill	37. A suspender	37. NOT GIVEN	37. B	37. C*
38. A propelled agitator	38. A concrete anchor	38. NO	38. sediment	38. E*
39. Vertical split moulds	39. TRUE	39. A reaction chamber	39. impact melt	39. G*
40. appearance	40. NOT GIVEN	40. residue	40. gases	40. B
				Note: Answers for qu. 36, 37, 38 + 39 in any order

READING ANSWERS HELP

This section shows fragments of passages that contain the correct answers. If you have trouble locating the correct answer in the text, or can't understand why a particular answer is correct, refer to this section to understand the reasoning behind the answers. A group of answers with answers being preceded by * means that this group of answers may be given in any order. Answers in brackets () are optional answers.

GENERAL READING TEST 1

1. **B**   2nd hand sales

2. **A**   *Sale on now - 25% off all sales of new computers*

3. **C**   This can range from teaching people to use a computer for the first time to programming courses

4. **F**   From the use of the ancient abacus to Lovelace and Babbage's 19th century work to code breaking in World War 2 to the development of the Internet. Come and learn how today's essential science, household and business tool was developed.

5. **E**   We'll show you how to beat slow connections

6. **A**   We also offer a complete set-up service

7. **C**   Check our online brochure for details of all our courses and fees

8. **TRUE**   The Beginner Diver Certificate takes place over three days

9. **TRUE**   For parties of six or more, we can offer attractive discounts.

10. **NOT GIVEN**   There is nothing in the text relating to this and so the answer is 'not given' in the text.

11. **FALSE**   The following medical issues might affect your eligibility to take our diving course: * Are you pregnant, or are you trying to get pregnant?

12. **FALSE**   Although we specialise in training new scuba divers, we run monthly advanced courses that cater for more experienced divers who wish to learn new skills and gain more advanced diving certification.

13. **NOT GIVEN**   There is nothing in the text relating to this and so the answer is 'not given' in the text.

14. **TRUE**   We are in contact with a variety of local hotels, guesthouses, bed and breakfasts, and even campsites or homestay households.

15. **time management**   It could be just public transport problems, but most of the time arriving late is because you didn't plan properly. Running late not only suggests poor time management skills, but shows a lack of respect for the company.

16. **dialogue**   A lot of candidates tend to think that an interview is the process of being asked questions. This is far from the truth, as both interviewer and interviewee ought to create a dialogue.

17. **products**   Therefore, prepare questions on the topics you're interested in. Ask questions about the company and their products.

18. **goals**   Try to understand what the organisation's goals are in the short, medium and long term and how the projects you'll work on will contribute.

19. **complainer**   don't ever say bad things about your current or previous employers in an interview. The interviewer will be listening to your answers and thinking about what it would be like to work with you. You may come across as a complainer

20. **competitive**   The job market is highly competitive and for every good position, there are usually a large number of candidates.

21. **smile**   Smile and show you're enjoying everything. Employers want to hire people who are passionate about their job and interested in their company.

22. **NO**   employees' average pay for the total hours worked mustn't fall below the National Minimum Wage.

23. **NO**   Unless an employee's contract guarantees them overtime, their employer can stop them from working it.

24. **NOT GIVEN**   There is nothing in the text relating to this and so the answer is 'not given' in the text.

25. **YES**   Employees who work overtime have to be paid a minimum of thirty minutes of work at overtime rates.

26. **YES**   Normally, most workers do not have to work on average more than forty-eight hours per week unless they agree. Even if they do agree, they have the right to opt out at any time by giving notice.

27. **NOT GIVEN**   There is nothing in the text relating to this and so the answer is 'not given' in the text.

28. **I**   Hunters applied facial and lip paint as means of camouflage.

29. **B**   Cosmetics, specifically lipstick, have captivated mankind since prehistoric times, mostly due to their ability to support people's individuality, improve their appearance and hence boost their confidence.

30. **E**   Because lip tissue lacks the pigment melanin, responsible for skin colour and the protection from ultraviolet rays, lipstick can protect the sensitive skin of lips from dry winds, moisture and sun.

31. **D**   From 2000 BC to 100 AD, ancient Mesopotamia and Egypt were the centres for cosmetics to develop, amongst others lipsticks and lip balms. It was at this time that carmine became a main constituent of lipstick.

32. **K**   it was only during the nineteenth century that they truly became publicly popular and accessible again. It was then that, due to industrial and technological advancements, French cosmetologists began the production of lipstick for commercial sales, which allowed the popularity of lipstick to reappear.

33. **J**   Lipstick ingredients have been under the spotlight recently, as discoveries by a US consumer group have found traces of the above-mentioned lead in several lipsticks exceeding regulations by the Food and Drug Administration (FDA). In tests, FDA scientists developed an analytical method for measuring the amount of lead in lipstick. Their findings confirmed that the amount of lead found in lipstick is very low and does not pose safety concerns. This did lead though to ingredient lists being required on lipstick packaging, much like is found on food.

34. **France**   Although cosmetics in France still retained popularity during the Middle Ages with the moneyed classes

35. **In the fridge**   Furthermore, preservatives, antioxidants and fragrance can be added, which is done in order to ensure a longer shelf life. This can also be done by storing it in the fridge. This prolongs the life of the lipstick in terms of delaying the degrading process of its ingredients.

36. **The cosmetics brands**   When creating a new lipstick, chemists need to consider the contemporary fashion mood. This also affects how the lipstick is presented to the public and its appearance is contingent on the requirements of the cosmetics brands.

37. **3-roll mill** the chosen pigment or a combination of pigments is mixed with various types of oils. A three-roll mill then grinds every particle

38. **A propelled agitator**   In the second stage, the pigment mixture is merged with wax, which is accomplished in a kettle surrounded by steam and powered by a propelled agitator.

39. **Vertical split moulds**   in order to get rid of 'cold-marks', which are unwanted products of fast cooling, the heated lipstick liquid at around eighty degrees Celsius is poured into vertical split moulds.

40. **appearance**   Finally, the lipstick is cooled down, taken out of the moulds and is prepared for flaming, a process that involves exposing the lipstick to an open flame. This ensures the better appearance of the lipstick and enhances its ability to protect itself from external influences such as air, moisture or heat.

GENERAL READING TEST 2

1. **E**   Because of this course's teaching and assessment structure, its fees are considerably less than all our other courses.

2. **D**   95% of our graduating students move from college to a job immediately and this more than anything shows how good our courses are.

3. **C**   This is a two-year full-time or three-year part-time course

4. **A**   You'll be taught by lecturers who are art and design experts, with experience in creative industries.

5. **C**   with three months in an appointment at a hotel or restaurant.

6. **C**   We always have many overseas students on this course and so students have access to special English support services if needed.

7. **B**   our students have ended up working in spas, 5-star resorts and on cruise liners.

8. **E**   Our full-time media course is completely taught and assessed online and students are free to choose how they study.

9. **F**   It has taken over from the Employment Service, which ran the previous Kenton Work Agency, Benefits Agency and Social Security office.

10. **B**   Whilst giving support to the unemployed, the personal advisors are also required to ensure that those claiming unemployment benefits are performing their obligations.

11. **D**   In addition young people can access the Training for Success programme. This is designed for young people aged 16 – 17, with extended eligibility up to age 22 for persons with a disability.

12. **C**   If you need help writing your CV, interview tips or maybe you could do with improving your literacy or numeracy skills, speak to the consultants in the Kenton Job Centre Plus Office, who will be happy to advise you.

13. **G**   Kenton Job Centre also offers assistance to Kenton employers. By informing the centre of their employee needs, the centre can find suitable candidates for the posts and employers are able to fill their vacancies quickly and successfully.

14. **H**   While taking part in Steps 2 Success, participants will continue to receive any Social Security benefits they are entitled to.

15. **line manager**   If that does not work, then a further stage can be tried. Speak to your line manager

16. **company website**   Our complaint procedure requires that a complaint should be made in writing and submitted to a member of the senior management. These people are clearly indicated on the company website.

17. **email address**   Employees must also supply their company email address.

18. **complaints meeting**   The appeal should again be done in writing. The general manager will instigate a complaints meeting, where the employee can give his position verbally and in writing.

19. **mediator**   If the employee still does not accept the decision, he or she can appeal again to the company director. If the director feels the appeal has merit, the case can be referred to an independent mediator.

20. **written record**   The managers involved are required to keep a written record of what happens during any complaint procedure. It is advised that employees do the same.

21. **footrest**   Have your knees level with your hips. You may need a footrest for this.

22. **cross**   Don't cross your legs, as this can cause posture-related problems.

23. **stand**   A good guide is to place the monitor about an arm's length away, with the top of the screen roughly at eye level. To achieve this, you may need to get a stand for your monitor.

24. **extended periods**   Consequently, there are particular muscles that will become tense when contracted in unnatural positions for extended periods.

25. **keyboard**   If you are not using your keyboard, push it to one side if using the mouse a lot.

26. **glare**   **Avoid screen glare.** Your screen should be as free of this as possible. If it's on your screen, hold a mirror in front of it to identify the cause. Position the monitor to avoid glare from overhead lighting and sunlight. If necessary, pull blinds across the windows and replace ceiling lighting with table lights.

27. **bifocals**   People with bifocals may find difficulties with computer work. It's important to be able to see the screen easily without having to raise or lower your head uncomfortably.

28. **E**   For this reason, there is a constant armed guard present at the bridge and this will also remain after completion.

29. **B**   One oddity of the bridge is that there is no pedestrian walkway on the bridge.

30. **A**   Due to all this, the building engineers decided to experiment and, instead of using a blimp or helicopter to drag the initial pilot link across the gorge, they used a rocket.

31. **D**   The bridge was meant to be a concrete beam bridge, but the lack of sand suitable for concrete in the area made this plan too expensive, as sand would have had to be transported to the building site. As a result, a suspension bridge was constructed

32. **C**   the road that created a safer and more direct route necessitated seven very high bridges and sixty-one tunnels; the Baluarte River Bridge is the highest of the bridges.

33. **B**   Some may argue that the Hegigio Gorge Bridge is not a true bridge, since it was not built for people, but for an oil pipeline.

34. **D**   The reason why Balinghe River Bridge has this unusual span size relates to the luck that the Chinese associate with the number 8, which sounds like the Mandarin word for "prosperity".

35. **B**   The first two hawsers were strung across by a helicopter

36. **E**   The bridge is not yet open

37. **A suspender**   The curving main steel cables also hold other cables (each is known as a suspender), which go down from the main steel cables to the road deck.

38. **A concrete anchor**   It is unusual in that, at each end, the main steel cables continue into the ground and are attached to a concrete anchor that provides extra stability and support.

39. **TRUE**   Another construction hurdle came from the harsh climate, which even today can be problematic to the operation of the pipeline.

40. **NOT GIVEN**   There is nothing in the text relating to this and so the answer is 'not given' in the text.

GENERAL READING TEST 3

1. **D**   If you've never done it before, coaching is available from the team of instructors.

2. **E**   Right now, there is a special short-term exhibit on the famous *Tyrannosaurus rex* from the New York Natural History Museum.

3. **B**   Just off the beach next to the car park, there's a snack café that serves cool or hot drinks and hot and cold meal options every day.

4. **F**   With thousands of titles to find (and borrow if you're a registered reader), you'll be sure of finding something of interest.

5. **C**   Visitors will be able to enjoy a variety of the exhibits and can also enjoy the hourly film on the history of motor transportation that's shown in The Visitors Centre.

6. **E**   Recently back in business after renovation

7. **A**   Guided tours available at 11 a.m. daily.

8. **F**   The library also has a range of computers connected to the internet, which anyone can use.

9. **D**   On Saturday mornings there are special kids sessions from opening time until midday.

10. **status**   Our discount card is available to anyone, though its price depends on the age and status of the person employed:

11. **driver**   Please note that you cannot buy the discount card on the buses themselves; a driver can only issue standard price travel tickets on the buses.

12. **photo**   If you buy your discount card in person, you don't need to provide a photo, as this can be done at any of our offices.

13. **register**   After purchase of your discount card, we strongly recommend that you register your card online on our website. This means that if your card is lost or stolen, it can be replaced free of charge and others will not be able to use your missing card.

14. **insurance**   Travellers are always advised to take out appropriate insurance when going on any foreign travel.

15. **TRUE**   Some pressure at work can act as motivation

16. **FALSE**   According to the government, last year 428,000 people reported work-related stress at a level they believed was making them ill. That's forty per cent of all work-related illness.

17. **TRUE**   Fierce emotions, jitters, sadness, or depression may all be part of this normal and usually temporary reaction to the stress of an overwhelming event.

18. **NOT GIVEN**   There is nothing in the text relating to this and so the answer is 'not given' in the text.

19. **FALSE**   Setting yourself goals and challenges, whether at work or outside, such as learning a new language or a new sport, helps to build confidence. That in turn will help you deal with stress.

20. **NOT GIVEN**   There is nothing in the text relating to this and so the answer is 'not given' in the text.

21. **TRUE**   *Whatever the source of your stress, speak to your line manager at Hayworth's. They all have training in assisting our workforce with any stress-related problems.*

22. **D**   The leave year and leave entitlement is not affected by new parent or adoption leave

23. **B**   How much leave a worker can carry over should be in the worker's contract.

24. **G**   An employer can turn down a leave request, but they must give as much notice as the amount of leave requested.

25. **A**   Public holidays can be different depending on the state or territory you work in.

26. **F**   Whether extra pay is due to a worker depends on the worker's contract, but this is not guaranteed.

27. **H**   An employee may have to take time off to care for an immediate family or household member who is sick or injured or help during a family emergency. This is known as carer's leave, but it comes out of the employee's personal leave balance.

28. **ii**   Various information within Paragraph A.

29. **i**   Various information within Paragraph B.

30. **viii**   Various information within Paragraph C.

31. **vi**   Various information within Paragraph D.

32. **v**   Various information within Paragraph E.

33. **x**   Various information within Paragraph F.

34. **vii**   Various information within Paragraph G.

35. **iii**   Various information within Paragraph H.

36. **YES**   Craven himself recommended aspirin for heart attack prevention in men between forty-five and sixty-five, who were overweight and sedentary, factors known to lead to heart attacks.

37. **NOT GIVEN**   There is nothing in the text relating to this and so the answer is 'not given' in the text.

38. **NO**   Also, although aspirin may be effective in preventing a stroke, it is important not to take aspirin when having a stroke.

39. **A reaction chamber**   It is made today by placing acetic anhydride and toluene in a mixing tank, before transferring the mixture to a reaction chamber, where salicylic acid is added and the chamber heated.

40. **Residue**   The exiting product is acetylsalicylic acid, which can then be converted to the form of aspirin that is required. Residue from filtration can be treated for a short while, before it can again be re-used in the process.

GENERAL READING TEST 4

1. **hoses**   Your new washing machine should not be installed in a place where temperatures may drop below 0° Celsius or the functioning of the electronic controls may not work properly and water hoses may burst or split.

2. **transit bars**   Before first use, ensure that the protective transit bars have been removed from the back of your new machine.

3. **ventilation**   If it is placed on a fitted or loose carpet, adjust the feet in such a way as to allow enough room for ventilation beneath the washing machine.

4. **flooding**   Ensure too that the drain line is secure or the force of the water exiting it may dislodge its position, which also can result in flooding.

5. **detergent**   Correct use of detergent will avoid the need for descaling

6. **energy consumption**   Water and energy consumption are linked to the size of your laundry load.

7. **landfill sites**   We hope to reduce the amount of non-recyclable waste that we send to landfill sites and increase recycling.

8. **plastic**   Because of this, please ensure no plastic is in your bio-waste or the fumes from it burning will pollute the air.

9. **on the pavement**   Rubbish bins ought to be put out on the pavement the night before the collection

10. **building waste**   The bulky service does not collect any building waste.

11. **using prepaid cards**   These points can be used to join a local rebate scheme with residents able to redeem their rewards using prepaid cards.

12. **FALSE**   Free initial consultation

13. **TRUE**   *Experts in conveyancing, wills, probate, power of attorney, migration and family law.*

14. **NOT GIVEN**   There is nothing in the text relating to this and so the answer is 'not given' in the text.

15. **liabilities**   You're 100% accountable for your business' liabilities, but you also retain full control of the business and its profits.

16. **same legal entity**   Many small business owners start out as sole traders, because sole traders aren't required to spend money following any formal or legal processes to establish their business, unlike companies. This is because sole traders and their businesses are considered to be the same legal entity.

17. **insolvent**   you can also be liable for business debts incurred by your partners if they become insolvent.

18. **partnership agreement**   Because partnerships entail more than one person in the decision-making process, it's important to discuss a wide variety of issues up front and develop a partnership agreement. This should document how future business decisions will be made, including how the partners will divide profits, resolve disputes, change ownership (bring in new partners or buy out current partners) and how to dissolve the partnership. Although they are not legally required, they are strongly recommended and it is considered extremely risky to operate without one.

19. **taxation**   Shareholder dividends undergo taxation at a different rate to the company itself.

20. **provisions**   However, you can include provisions in your operating agreement to prolong the life of the company if a member decides to leave the business.

21. **FALSE**   If you find that you are paying out of your own pocket more money than your personal finances can deal with, please get in contact with your line manager immediately and he/she will ensure that you are repaid immediately.

22. **TRUE**   When an expense is reimbursed, the Department of Taxation must be satisfied that the expense is allowable for tax purposes. If not, the repayment from an employer is treated as extra taxable income.

23. **TRUE**   Examples of items you can claim for while on company business: ... Hotel bills and meals there

24. **NOT GIVEN**   There is nothing in the text relating to this and so the answer is 'not given' in the text.

25. **TRUE**   If you use your own Internet connection, then you may only claim a proportion of the bill based on your company usage.

26. **NOT GIVEN**   There is nothing in the text relating to this and so the answer is 'not given' in the text.

27. **FALSE**   The company can reimburse you for some expenses without proof of payment, but we try and keep this to a minimum.

28. **B**   Meteorites commonly collide with Earth, but the majority are destroyed in the impact with the Earth's atmosphere.

29. **D** The Alvarez Hypothesis theorises ... and shrouding the globe for years in a thick cocoon of sky-blackening dust and debris.

30. **C** The limestone outside of Gubbio, which was once below the sea, provides total geological evidence of the end of the Cretaceous period and the beginning of the Tertiary period.

31. **B** This time span is sometimes referred to as "the Great Dying," because a massive extinction claimed nearly seventy-five per cent of all the species of life on our planet

32. **B** The clay layer itself contained no marine fossils at all.

33. **D** To the amazement of everyone involved, the measurements showed that the clay layer was about six hundred times richer in iridium than the surrounding limestone.

34. **C** These same iridium results were subsequently also discovered in clay layers at locations in Denmark and New Zealand, and later dozens of other sites around the world where the geological record of the Cretaceous-Tertiary boundaries is also complete. These iridium-spiked layers of clay also contained an abundance of soot.

35. **D** This paper was immediately resisted by scientific critics

36. **F** First, there was the discovery of shocked quartz along with the iridium and soot in the clay layer samples from around the world, which could only have been produced in the heat and violence of a titanic smash. Second came the discovery in 1991 of the scene of the titanic smash - the Chicxulub crater. This meteorite impact was thought to have caused the broken up quartz.

37. **B** The discovery of this impact site answered critics of the Alvarez Hypothesis who'd been demanding to know: if an asteroid impact killed the dinosaurs, where's the crater?

38. **sediment** The crater nowadays is buried beneath a thousand meters of sediment.

39. **impact melt** Under this is a layer of what is known as impact breccias and then a deposit of the impact melt.

40. **gases** Beneath that is the rock that was needed to be brought to surface for research. The rock was shown to be made of anhydrite, which is a mineral that, if it were vaporised in an impact event, would produce the particular gases that could alter the Earth's weather.

GENERAL READING TEST 5

1. **D**   Drop your car off with us today

2. **E**   I can also iron, launder, cook and babysit.

3. **B**   *Same day service available.*

4. **F**   A badly maintained chimney can cause excessive dirt and a risk of fire.

5. **C**   Fully insured

6. **E**   I can supply lots of genuine references with telephone numbers for you to double-check.

7. **C**   or contact him on handyandy@living.com

8. **NOT GIVEN**   There is nothing in the text relating to this and so the answer is 'not given' in the text.

9. **FALSE**   You can join also online and then pick up your library card one day later when you visit us and show us your ID.

10. **NOT GIVEN**   There is nothing in the text relating to this and so the answer is 'not given' in the text.

11. **TRUE**   10 books or audiobooks for 4 weeks + You can renew items for a further 2 weeks

12. **FALSE**   If you want a book or journal article that the library does not hold, you can request it free of charge through Inter Library Loans.

13. **TRUE**   Booking can only be done in person or by telephone.

14. **TRUE**   Singing the songs with your baby in this environment can help with their speech development, sense of timing, confidence and social skills.

15. **(technical) knowledge**   Having a website for a business today is a must, though some people shy away from it because they fear the expense and feel they are short of the technical knowledge.

16. **consultation**   We will start with a consultation with you to find out what you require.

17. **worldwide traders**   Not every business operates their selling online, but if you want this option, we have lots of experience with setting up a system that will suit you. We can cover all types of business, from beginners to worldwide traders.

18. **unexpected charges**   We have various transparent packages that you can choose from. We never lock you into a contract, so you can withdraw at any time or change your package without incurring any unexpected charges.

19. **sales executives** Operating a website on the Internet nowadays means marketing it hard through all aspects of social media, online PR and what is known as search engine optimisation. We can train you in all this or do a lot of it for you. It's a complex business, so contact one of our sales executives who can give details on what you need to know and how exactly we can help you.

20. **dynamic**   Nowadays, businesses are tremendously dynamic and we understand that you will want to change your website from time to time.

21. **website code**   Your relative security is high if you have few network resources of financial value, your company and site aren't controversial in any way, your network is set up with tight permissions, your web server is patched up to date with all settings done correctly, your applications on the web server are all patched and updated, and your website code is done to high standards.

22. **Their first day**   All our staff accrue paid sick leave (PSL) from their first day.

23. **The absence manager**   When you realise that you feel too ill to come to work, you should please call the absence manager as soon as you can.

24. **The following weekend** we have a policy that states that if you call in sick at the weekend, you have to come in the following weekend.

25. **disabilities**   If you have developed any disabilities during your sickness, we are obliged to make reasonable adjustments to your work conditions

26. **8 months**   After eight months, we can dismiss an employee who is long-term sick

27. **An employment tribunal**   *You can take your case to an employment tribunal if you think you've been unfairly dismissed.*

28. **MW**   Mary Winters sums up her clients' feelings. "The image of a screw cap is firmly lodged in many minds as the epitome of cheap wine.

29. **JC**   Wine connoisseur, Jean Costaud, says it also adds to the wine experience. "It's all to do with when the wine is opened. No artificial stopper can come close to reproducing the iconic "pop" when the cork is removed."

30. **AD**   American wine producer, Alice Deacon, is more interested in the second, more technical problem. "We want to know whether the synthetic material is truly non-reactive and inert over long periods of time. Will it impart any tastes of its own to the wine?"

31. **SM**   Sally Marshall, explains why. "Cork's success as a closure depends upon its fitting snugly into an opening with a relatively uniform diameter. Thus, it was not until the seventeenth century, when glass bottles were first made with openings more or less the same size, that the cork truly came into its own."

32. **MB**   Mike Baker, a CEO at a footwear company, is a big fan. "The transformation of used wine corks into durable and attractive footwear is an easy and elegant way to extend the life-cycle of this remarkable material

33. **JC**   Jean Costaud explains the problem. "A lightly corked wine may simply smell like cork, while a badly corked wine smells musty, like damp cardboard or old newspapers. The usual rich aroma and taste of the wine is stripped away by the musty odor."

34. **CW**   Environmentalist, Charles Wrathe, explains. "It seems like a small thing, but every cork stopper represents a carbon offset of 113.5 grams. Looked at differently, the 6.6 million acres of Mediterranean cork oaks capture approximately 14.4 million metric tons of carbon dioxide."

35. **JR**   Jose Rivera, a Portuguese cork grower, explains. "While it might seem counterintuitive, the best way to ensure that there is no shortage of cork is to use more cork. That is because the greater the demand for cork, the greater the economic incentive there will be to protect the cork oak forests for future generations."

36. **B***   With all the beneficial properties of corks as bottle closures, there is one significant defect. This is "corkiness", a condition that exists when wine is tainted by the presence of a chemical compound called 2, 4, 6 - Trichloroanisole - TCA for short. This compound appears to be caused in the cork by the interaction of moisture, chlorine and mould that is always there.

37. **C***   An artificial cork is made of ethylene vinyl acetate. It looks and feels very similar to real cork and a corkscrew is used to remove it from the bottle.

38. **E***   Nonetheless, more and more low- and mid-range producers are switching to an artificial cork.

39. **G***   Amazingly, cork floor tiles are a great product. They are lightweight, permeable, physically resilient and chemically inert.

40. **B**   This is a holistic answer and involves synthesis of the whole text. This text in its entirety fits "Cork: A versatile Material" better than the other three answers.

EXAMPLE WRITING ANSWERS

Below you will find example writing answers for all the writing questions in the General Practice Tests 1 to 5. There are many ways of answering the writing questions and these examples are only one possibility of a good answer. Please refer to the question papers while you are reading these letters and essays so that you understand the questions that are being answered. We hope this will give you an insight into how the writing answers should be written for IELTS General module in order to get a Band 8 - 8.5.

GENERAL WRITING PRACTICE TEST 1

Task 1

Dear Sir / Madam,

I am writing to you to express my interest in your job advertisement for a chef that I saw posted on the local village board. As I have currently moved to Brenton as a qualified chef, I would therefore like to apply for this position.

I noticed from the job description that you require someone who can both cook in a creative and healthy way, and who can communicate with and manage staff in an effective manner. My previous job was as an assistant chef at Brew's restaurant in London, where I was responsible for preparing all the dishes on the restaurant's menu and coming up with inventive recipes to present to the head chef. I am also personally very interested in healthy living and this is always reflected in how I cook. I was also responsible at Brew's for managing the cleaning and serving staff at the restaurant, in which capacity I found I was able to build good working relationships with all the staff in my responsibility.

I noticed that this is a part-time job. My preferred days for working would be Monday, Wednesday and Friday afternoons and evenings. I would be available until late at night on those days and I would also be able to work two Saturdays of each month.

I look forward to hearing from you soon. Please let me know if you require any further information.

Yours sincerely,

Marisa Thompson

(241 words)

Task 2

Humans have become a prime culprits for the destruction of the wildlife population around the world. Humans believe that they are the most powerful species on this planet and have therefore chosen to use all of nature's resources for their own good, even if this results in the destruction of the environment around them. Clearly, this is not a positive result of human existence and many people believe that the world's wildlife population should be better protected.

One possible way to protect wildlife around the world is to reduce the amount of polluted substances produced through the human way of life. It has become habitual for people to pollute water by adding chemicals to it during industrial processes or to pollute air as a result of the fossil fuel industries and car emissions. Stopping the addition of chemicals to water and creating cleaner processes would reduce water pollution and help create a safer environment for wildlife to live in. Increasing the availability and use of public transportation and increasing the use of renewable energy sources could reduce world pollution further.

Another possible attempt to protect wildlife around the world is to actively promote recycling projects to reduce the amount of resources that are wasted. This would lessen the degradation of the natural environment, as humans continue to search for new resources. Society uses a lot of paper and wood on a daily basis and people do not actively think about whether or not they are wasting these resources. Printing double-sided or on recycled paper for example would appear to change nothing, yet if carried out regularly would help make a difference.

In conclusion, there are numerous different ways in which every human being can help to protect the wildlife population around the world. One can engage in projects to raise awareness of environmental destruction or one can actively take part in activities to protect it. Everyone must find the area in which he or she would like to involve him or herself, as all should be obliged to protect wildlife around the world.

(343 words)

GENERAL WRITING PRACTICE TEST 2

Task 1

Dear Sarah,

Now that the weekend of my birthday party is over and you have hopefully arrived home safely, I just wanted to let you know again how much your birthday present means to me. I don't think I've ever received something quite as original as this lovely, hand-made photo album with photos and notes reminding me of our childhood. I think that these memories have helped us stick together and I hope that, although we live a long way apart now, I can add to this album every year when we see each other. With the stationery collection that my mother gave me and the calligraphy set I got from my dad, I can easily continue to add to this work of art!

It's sad that you could only be there for the party and not for my actual birthday. I went canoeing with my parents and my sister at Barley Creek, the lovely lake resort that we often used to go to when we were young. Do you remember the tall trees and the calm atmosphere there? Well, everything is still as it used to be. Even the castle restaurant is still there, where I topped the day off with a fancy dinner. What a memorable day it was!

I hope you can be there next time.

Lots of love,

Amara

(223 words)

Task 2

In modern day society, education has become a vital aspect of every child's life. Educational facilities tend to offer a wide range of subjects aimed at educating children and teaching them various skills. Fundamental subject areas are said to be mathematics, science, languages and physical education. Whilst some have the ideology that musical education is an important part of growing up, others believe that it should no longer be taught in schools, as it is considered a waste of time and resources. In my view, it is important to incorporate music in children's education as it promotes creativity.

Typically people judge that learning to express oneself in a creative manner is less important than learning about mathematical theories and scientific facts. Music falls under the subject area of art, causing it to often be considered as less valuable than other subjects. Often the opponents of musical education propose that a more rationally-based education will benefit children later on in their lives, as they will be able to perceive and comprehend the logical aspects of life more easily.

The supporters of musical education, on the other hand, argue that music is beneficial for children, because it offers a manner of creative self-expression. It is important for a child to learn about thinking creatively and to take a break from logical subjects once in a while. Furthermore, music is a salient part of human culture, as it brings people together and therefore children who study music can obtain a sense of cultural knowledge.

In conclusion, music should be taught at school, because it enables children to express themselves creatively and to learn more about culture and human interaction. I, personally, benefited from musical education, because I played piano for seven years and believe that this has helped me become a more balanced person.

(301 words)

GENERAL WRITING PRACTICE TEST 3

Task 1

Dear Sir / Madam,

My family and I have just recently been a guest at Seaside Resort in a rented apartment. Even though the view overlooking the sea was lovely, several things in the apartment were missing or unsatisfactory and I would like to use this opportunity to explain the problems leading to this complaint.

First of all, the wooden steps leading up to the door of the apartment did not meet official security standards: one step broke when my husband carried our luggage up, leaving him with a bruised leg, and two other steps were also dangerously close to breaking apart in the middle. Additionally, when my children wanted to put away their clothes in the available cupboards, one of the planks broke loose, hitting my younger son and scaring both children. Finally, the kitchen did not have enough cutlery, let alone cups, and the sink in the bathroom only worked after my husband worked on it.

As you can see, the condition of the apartment was unsatisfactory in many ways, and I would therefore like to ask for a discount of thirty per cent of the price we paid for the rent.

I hope this feedback was useful to you and will help to make Seaside Resort a better place for tourists in the future. Please report back to me regarding your plans of how to deal with this situation!

Yours sincerely,

Mrs. Angela Driftwood

(237 words)

Task 2

The wearing of school uniforms is an issue that is both supported and opposed by many people. Numerous schools around the world require students to wear school uniforms on their grounds, however, teachers are not often required to wear a specific uniform while working. It has therefore been suggested that it should be compulsory for teachers to wear a specific uniform or follow a specific dress code on a daily basis.

One reason for introducing a dress code for teachers would be that teachers typically function as role models. For students who are not willing to conform to the dress code of their school, it would be beneficial to see figures of authority wearing the same outfit as each other, and they would then potentially be more willing to follow their own dress code.

Another reason for introducing a compulsory dress code for teachers would be that if all teachers wore the same outfit, there would be no visible difference amongst them. Naturally some teachers are wealthier than others and would tend to show this through their clothing. This could cause other teachers to feel inferior and therefore could result in lower quality work and decreased motivation. Furthermore, students would feel treated more fairly, if not only they, but teachers as well had to wear a certain uniform in school.

Lastly, uniforms for teachers would enable students and other teachers to easily distinguish between school staff and other adults. In many schools there is no high quality security system and strangers can easily enter and steal something or commit other crimes. If teachers wore uniforms, one would then be able to approach and confront strangers more easily, as one could distinguish teachers wearing uniforms clearly from other adults.

In conclusion, there are many positive effects of introducing uniforms for teachers and therefore, in my opinion, they should be installed in as many schools as possible.

(315 words)

GENERAL WRITING PRACTICE TEST 4

Task 1

Dear Sir / Madam,

My name is Amanda Rosewell and I am a resident of the city of Harpley. I am writing this letter in my name and on behalf of my neighbours on Bristwood Avenue, as we have experienced very poor rubbish collection services recently.

For around three months, the trash I put out at my gate on the correct day is only collected irregularly, and when it is, some is left behind. My neighbours have had similar experiences, if not worse, with one woman not having her rubbish collected for eight weeks and another family dealing with unfriendly and incompetent rubbish collectors. Apparently, their waste container was broken by the harsh handling of the collectors, and the family's children have been scared by their unfriendly comments.

Although I have called the rubbish collection service hotline, the company's employees have not taken my complaint seriously and nothing has changed the current situation. I would therefore like to ask what you as the local city council can do in order to improve this state of affairs, as the rubbish collection services do not react to any feedback from dissatisfied citizens.

I look forward to hearing from you soon.

Yours sincerely,

Amanda Rosewell

(202 words)

Task 2

In modern day western society one can easily become obese, as the availability of cheap and unhealthy food is high. Nonetheless, many people desire to be healthy and slim and therefore have chosen to follow special diets or exercise regimes so as to not become obese. Others believe, however, that people should be better informed about today's unhealthy lifestyles and the poor food they are consuming before such diets and regimes are taken into consideration. Personally, I agree that the unhealthy lifestyle of many people must be addressed before thinking about ways of losing weight through special diets.

It has become habitual for people to cook using ingredients that have been pre-cooked or to which chemicals have been added. Additionally, many people consume a lot of microwave and fast food, which are both easy to purchase and prepare, but are often fairly unhealthy. Due to the fact that it has become less popular to cook meals using fresh ingredients, people consume chemicals, taste intensifiers, salt and sugar without realising. By consuming food that has been made by mass production, one no longer has to think carefully about how a meal is prepared and can simply consume it without thinking about the ingredients.

It seems logical that in order to lose weight effectively and over a long period of time, one has to learn to eat in a healthy way and to carry out sport on a regular basis. Learning how to cook with fresh ingredients is an important aspect of eating in a healthy way, and, by doing so, people can avoid eating food that has been pre-made. If people do not understand this concept, they will fall back into unhealthily habits after their diet is over.

In conclusion, today's unhealthy lifestyles as well as the poor quality food consumed by people on a regular basis must be addressed before thinking about diets or exercise regimes. If people can combine exercise with wholesome eating habits, they will be happier and healthier.

(331 words)

GENERAL WRITING PRACTICE TEST 5

Task 1

Dear John,

I have recently been given a trip to France as a reward for my hard work at my company, and I may choose someone to come with me.

As you studied French at university and are therefore not only familiar with the language, but also the culture, I'd love it if you could come with me. I'm sure you'll enjoy the holiday, as you do not just have to translate, but you can also appreciate the beauties of France with me.

We will leave Toronto on the third of September and will fly back on the nineteenth. In France we will arrive in Paris, we will stay there for four days and then take a bus to see the Provence region for around three days. From there, we will take the train to Marseille and Cannes, as these are the most popular cities in the south. Finally, one of my colleagues will take us back to Paris by car, as he is going there on a business trip. We will only need to have spending money as flights, other travel and accommodation are all included.

There are a few things I'd like to see, for example the Louvre museum in Paris, the Chateau of Versailles and the Picasso Museum in the south of France. I hope you'll have some ideas as well.

Please tell me if you are interested in this trip. I would really appreciate having you as company and I look forward to hearing back from you!

Best wishes,

Christopher

(254 words)

Task 2

In recent years it has become normal for high school graduates to travel abroad for their university education. There are numerous positive aspects to studying in a foreign country, such as the discovery of new cultures, the possibility of learning more about oneself and the chance of learning a new language.

By travelling to a foreign country, it is certain that one will be confronted with foreign customs and traditions. Experiencing and understanding these customs and their origins provides students with an interesting chance to develop a more open-minded attitude towards others. Additionally, it is also extremely stimulating to learn more about the reasons behind certain traditions and practices.

A prime reason for students studying abroad is the prospect of finding oneself and growing as an individual. When living in a foreign country, students have to become increasingly independent and they are confronted with their strengths and weaknesses. Typically students develop increased self-esteem and also acquire or improve upon their skills of housekeeping and cooking, which are important for living independently later on in life.

When living in a foreign country students are exposed to a new language and in most cases attempt to learn it. If they already possess some knowledge about the language, they have the possibility of advancing and improving upon these skills with the native population. The ability to speak multiple languages offers students a higher chance of being successful on the international job market, which makes studying abroad an attractive choice.

Personally, I would like to study abroad in either Scotland or France, because I would like to experience the life and customs in these countries. Additionally, I would like to become more fluent in French, as I believe this will be beneficial for me later on in life.

In conclusion, studying abroad offers the possibility for students to grow and develop as an individual and to acquire valuable skills that will be useful later on in life.

(323 words)

COMMENTARY ON THE EXAMPLE SPEAKING RECORDINGS

In this section you will find reports by an IELTS speaking examiner on the recordings of
Speaking Tests 1 - 5. The questions asked in the recordings are the questions in the Speaking Tests 1 –
5, so, while listening to the recordings, it is advised to have the questions with you for reference. The
recordings are not real IELTS test recordings, but the interviewer is a real IELTS examiner and the
recordings are conducted in the exact way that an IELTS Speaking Test is done.

SPEAKING PRACTICE TEST 1

Examiner's Commentary

The person interviewed is Clara, a French female. Clara is a teacher.

Part 1

Clara spoke fluently and confidently. She showed that she had an excellent vocabulary range with only
very occasional mildly awkward word choices. She showed she could speak at length and on varied topics
without needing to pause to access words or grammar, though there were some occasional hesitations.
One grammar slip came up when she said "since a long time" rather than 'for a long time.'

Part 2

Clara spoke well in Part 2. She had no problem with speaking long enough, even though she did not use
all the preparation time given. Clara again showed her fluency and accuracy with no pauses and few
errors (she said "inconvenient" once instead of 'inconvenience' and she had one missed article). Clara also
showed a sense of humour, which is a nice touch in a speaking test. She justified herself well without
pausing with the unexpected question at the end.

Part 3

Again, Clara spoke fluently and accurately and again showed humour. She spoke formally, though
occasionally used some informal vocabulary at suitable points. Clara was good at giving full answers, for
example, she gave a good list of both advantages and disadvantages of owning a car. In spite of more
demanding questions, Clara showed little hesitation and used more complex grammar flexibly and
accurately. There were only very occasional errors ("pushing foot down" instead of 'putting' and "consider
stop driving" instead of 'consider stopping') and she coped well when searching for a word she didn't
know – using "degrees" for alcohol testing, which was perfectly comprehensible.

Marking - The marking of the IELTS Speaking Test is done in 4 parts.

Fluency and Coherence	8
Lexical Resource	8
Grammatical Range and Accuracy	8
Pronunciation	8
Estimated IELTS Speaking Band	**8**

SPEAKING PRACTICE TEST 2

Examiner's Commentary

The person interviewed is Darija, a Croatian female. Darija is a personal assistant.

Part 1

Darija showed that she had a good command of English. Her speech was very clear and there was an American accent apparent. She showed excellent fluency (she got tongue-tied once – not a problem) and gave full answers to all questions. There were no grammar errors and only the very occasional minor awkward word choice.

Part 2

Darija showed again that her English is fluent, accurate and idiomatic. She had few pauses in her long turn and only occasional fluency trips. There was one grammar error at the end ("than we used to" instead of 'than we are used to').

Part 3

Darija again showed her excellent command of English with her good and full answers. She was fluent and accurate with only occasional fluency trips and grammar slips ("the nature" instead of 'nature'). Darija's lexical range is excellent, with only the occasional awkward word choice.

Marking - The marking of the IELTS Speaking Test is done in 4 parts.

Fluency and Coherence	8
Lexical Resource	8
Grammatical Range and Accuracy	8
Pronunciation	9

Estimated IELTS Speaking Band   **8**

SPEAKING PRACTICE TEST 3

Examiner's Commentary

The person interviewed is Yi Xhuen, a Chinese female. Yi Xhuen is a student.

Part 1

Yi Xhuen spoke slowly, but reasonably clearly. She lacked the intonation an English native speaker has and this made her often sound rather wooden. Her pronunciation was fair, but there were some words that were unclear or poorly pronounced (e.g. serious). Yi Xhuen's vocabulary was reasonable, but she lacked range. She was, however, quite good at 'talking round' something and making herself understood when she lacked the words. There were errors though (e.g. "It is over population" instead of 'over-populated'). Yi Xhuen had reasonable grammatical accuracy, but again had a limited range.

Part 2

Yi Xhuen took the preparation time available to her, and this is always strongly recommended – there's no advantage to not taking the time. Yi Xhuen was more hesitant with the challenge of the demands of speaking for so long in Part 2 and her fluency was affected. Sometimes she talked herself into a corner and found it difficult to get out. There were also more errors in grammar and word choice. In spite of all this, Yi Xhuen spoke for the required amount of time and made herself understood on different topics and she also showed a sense of humour.

Part 3

Yi Xhuen was able to cope with the more demanding questions of Part 3, but her answers could have been longer and more developed. She still showed the intonation, fluency and pronunciation problems of the earlier Parts and the more complex topics caused more hesitancy and pauses. She also made more grammar errors, some quite basic ("My country suffer" instead of "My country suffers" – 3rd person agreement). On the other hand, Yi Xhuen spoke for the required amount of time and answered all questions properly and sometimes with examples. Yi Xhuen could certainly always communicate what she wanted to say. Overall, Yi Xhuen's ability in everything was fair, but lacked range and flexibility.

Yi Xhuen's English in Part 3 was much the same as before. She managed to answer each question fully and without too much hesitation, but her grammar and vocabulary ranges were limited and her pronunciation was heavily influenced by her mother tongue. Yi Xhuen has a few limitations in her English, but she can certainly communicate fairly well.

Marking - The marking of the IELTS Speaking Test is done in 4 parts.

Fluency and Coherence	5
Lexical Resource	5
Grammatical Range and Accuracy	6
Pronunciation	4
Estimated IELTS Speaking Band	**5**

SPEAKING PRACTICE TEST 4

Examiner's Commentary

The person interviewed is Welta, a Thai female. Welta works in a shop.

Part 1

Welta addressed all the questions, but there were some problems with all aspects of her English. Her Thai accent was very apparent and this often interfered with communication. For example, the problem with her pronunciation of "r" made her English sound awkward and strange. Some lexis, on the other hand, were pronounced very clearly. Welta had to pause fairly frequently to access ideas and lexis, which affected her fluency. In general, Welta did not give long enough answers. She needed to try and develop most of her answers, so that she could demonstrate a wider range of lexis and grammatical structure. Welta also often misses out words in a sentence, but is confident to carry on, as the words that she does produce usually communicate her meaning.

Part 2

The problems identified in Part 1 were again apparent. Welta did manage to include some details, however, and managed to talk for over a minute. There were various grammatical and syntactical problems, for example her use of articles. Welta spoke fairly slowly and seemed to lack confidence.

Part 3

With the added difficulty of Part 3, Welta's performance worsened. The lexis, grammar range and flexibility of thought in English required to deal with the questions were often beyond her English language ability, though she attempted to answer everything. The answers and therefore the entire Part were far too short.

Marking - The marking of the IELTS Speaking Test is done in 4 parts.

Fluency and Coherence	4
Lexical Resource	4
Grammatical Range and Accuracy	4
Pronunciation	4

Estimated IELTS Speaking Band   **4**

SPEAKING PRACTICE TEST 5

Examiner's Commentary

The person interviewed is Eva, a Latvian female. Eva is a teacher.

Part 1

Eva spoke fluently and accurately in this Part. She has an accent, but it does not obstruct communication. Eva has a very good vocabulary range and accurate grammar usage. There was one error (i.e. "from Internet" instead of 'from the Internet'), but it was extremely minor. She provided good full answers and only paused to think about good answers for questions.

Part 2

Eva did not need the preparation time, which was available. She performed fine, but I would not recommend not using the time given. Eva was fluent and accurate and used a very good and natural vocabulary range. The accent was still apparent, but did not hinder understanding. Eva did not make any grammar errors.

Part 3

Eva again showed excellent fluency, grammar and vocabulary range. The accent is still there, but again it does not stop communication or understanding.

Marking - The marking of the IELTS Speaking Test is done in 4 parts.

Fluency and Coherence	8
Lexical Resource	8
Grammatical Range and Accuracy	8
Pronunciation	7

Estimated IELTS Speaking Band   8

Listening Recordings' Transcripts

LISTENING TEST 1 TRANSCRIPT

This recording is copyright by Robert Nicholson and Simone Braverman, all rights reserved.

IELTS listening practice tests. Test one. In the IELTS test you hear some recordings and you have to answer questions on them. You have time to read the instructions and questions and check your work. All recordings are played only once. The test is in four parts. Now turn to part one.

Part one. You will hear a conversation between a man and a woman discussing lost property at a cinema.

First you have some time to look at questions one to five.

(20 second gap)

Now we begin. You should answer the questions as you listen, as the recording is not played twice. Listen carefully to the conversation and answer questions one to five.

Peter	Good morning. Do you work here at this cinema?
Angela	Yes, I do. My name's Angela. Can I help you?
Peter	I was here last night watching a film and I think I dropped my wallet under my seat.
Angela	Oh, I don't have the keys for the lost property drawer. I can take some information for you and I'll get Mr. <u>Smith</u> to call you when he comes in. He's in charge of lost property.
Peter	That'll be fine.
Angela	What's your name?
Peter	Peter Simpson. Simpson is spelled <u>S - I - M - P - S - O – N</u> **(Q1)**.
Angela	And can you let me know your address?
Peter	I live at <u>thirteen</u> **(Q2)**. Winchester Road, Alton.
Angela	And the postcode?
Peter	It's W twelve,<u> seven RT</u>. **(Q3)**
Angela	Now, I need a contact telephone number for you.
Peter	I'll give you my mobile number, as that'll be more convenient. It's oh one seven four three, oh six two, four nine six.
Angela	Thanks. Now, what film were you watching?
Peter	It was the new Spiderman movie.

Angela	What showing did you see?

Peter   It was the one that began at <u>seven-thirty p.m.</u> **(Q4)**.

Angela   Do you remember where you were sitting?

Peter   Yes. I still have my ticket. Here it is. I was in seat <u>F twenty-three</u> **(Q5)**. There was only one other person near me in G twenty-four, so my wallet shouldn't have been found by another customer.

Angela   Thanks.

Before the conversation continues, you have some time to look at questions six to ten.

(20 second gap)

Now listen carefully and answer questions six to ten.

Angela   Now, could you give me some details about the contents of your wallet?

Peter   Well, I had <u>some cash, around twenty pounds I think</u> **(Q6-Q10)**. Then there were my bank cards, <u>my debit card, and credit cards</u> **(Q6-Q10)**.

Angela   Have you cancelled them yet?

Peter   Yes, I did that this morning when I realised that my wallet was missing. I don't keep a note of the PIN numbers in my wallet, so the cards should be safe.

Angela   Anything else?

Peter   <u>My company ID is in there</u> **(Q6-Q10)**. That's a card that I swipe when I go into work. I usually have my company photocopy card in there as well, but for some reason I left that on my desk.

Angela   OK. I've made a note of that.

Peter   Next week, <u>I'm coming back to the cinema for another film. I bought the ticket last night, so that is in the wallet too</u> **(Q6-Q10)**. I'm also going to the theatre, but that ticket is in the glove compartment of my car.

Angela   Anything else? We've had people who lost wallets with hotel card keys, library cards, health insurance cards, passports and lots of other things.

Peter   Yes, you're right. <u>I do have my health insurance card in there</u> **(Q6-Q10)**. I'd forgotten. But that's it.

Angela   Right then. Thanks very much, Mr. Simpson. I'm sorry I can't tell you more right now, but I'll give this information to Mr. Smith the moment he gets in and I'll make sure he calls right away.

Peter   Thanks very much. Goodbye.

Angela   Goodbye.

That is the end of part one. You will now have half a minute to check your answers.

(30 second gap)

Now turn to part two.

Part two. You will hear a woman telling some people about the organisation of a conference. First you have some time to look at questions eleven to fifteen.

(20 second gap)

Now listen carefully to the information talk and answer questions eleven to fifteen.

Good morning and welcome to this first talk of the conference on the conservation of natural resources. My name is Linda. Before we start with our first official speaker, I'd like to tell you a little about the organisation of the event.

First of all, I'd like to tell you that within the conference areas, all your food and non-alcoholic drinks are free, as the costs have been included within the price of your ticket. All you need to do is to show the blue identification card that you were issued when you registered. If you wear it round your neck with the string provided, then it is easily seen and not easy to lose. If you do lose it, please come to see me at my catering desk with some identification and I'll issue you a new one. As you came into the conference area earlier through the main entrance, you will have seen a large rectangular room, which is the conference reception room. The catering desk is in this room, just to the right of the conference entrance as you come in **(Q11)**. If you have not yet officially registered, you can do that at the registration desk across the room directly opposite my catering desk **(Q12)**. Again, just bring a piece of identification.

We know that some of you will not have yet organised anywhere to stay. If you'd like some help with that, you can visit our accommodation desk, which is found to the left of the registration desk as you come into the conference reception room **(Q13)**. The bathrooms are between these two desks. We have agreed some special rates at some nearby hotels that also have free shuttle services to and from this conference centre. You won't find a better deal.

During the conference, there will be two speeches going on at any one time. After the opening speech that follows my talk, you can choose to stay in this hall, which is Lancaster Hall, or go to the other hall, which is Kensington Hall. Lancaster Hall, which is the one we are in right now, is through the only door in the right hand wall of the conference reception room **(Q14)** and Kensington Hall is directly opposite **(Q15)**. Plans and schedules are available on the desk on the left of the conference reception room entrance as you come in. Please help yourself.

You now have some time to look at questions sixteen to twenty.

(20 second gap)

Now listen to the rest of the information talk and answer questions sixteen to twenty.

And now, before the opening speech, I'd like to tell you about the refreshments organised for this event.

In the mornings before the first speeches, we will have tea, coffee, juices and water along with <u>some fruit</u> **(Q16)** available on tables. Please help yourselves, but please don't take food or drinks into the conference halls. Just leave used crockery on the tables provided.

Lunches will be served in the conference centre's restaurant. To get there, leave our conference area and go up to <u>the second floor</u> **(Q17)** by lift, escalator or stairs. You will see the restaurant there easily. In the restaurant, the food will be served cafeteria style, so that the large number of people can be handled efficiently. There will be starters, soups and salads available as well as main courses. The main course will have two meat options, one vegetarian option and <u>one</u> **(Q18)** vegan option. There will be the usual side dishes such as potatoes, pasta, rice and a range of vegetables. There will also be a choice of deserts and fruit to finish your meal. Drinks are also available in the restaurant. As I said before, everything soft will be free of charge, but you will have to pay extra for things like wine and beer. Tea and coffee will be available in the restaurant as well.

In the afternoon, we will serve tea in the conference area. However, if the weather is good, we will serve the tea <u>on the terrace</u> **(Q19)**. Tea, coffee, juices and water will be available to drink and to eat there will be a selection of sandwiches, cakes and biscuits. These will be laid out for you, so just help yourselves.

If you have any queries or complaints, please come and see me. In the morning and afternoons, I will be at the catering desk and at lunchtimes, I will be stationed <u>in the restaurant</u> **(Q20)**.

I'll stop now and hand you over to our first official speaker.

That is the end of part two. You will now have half a minute to check your answers.

(30 second gap)

Now turn to part three.

Part three. You will hear a student and a lecturer discussing a university course on coastal erosion. First you have some time to look at questions twenty-one to twenty-five.

(20 second gap)

Now listen carefully and answer questions twenty-one to twenty-five.

Amanda	Good morning, Dr. Peters. Can I ask you a couple of questions?
Dr. Peters	Oh, good morning, Amanda. Yes, I'm free right now. Go ahead.
Amanda	I wanted to ask you about the course that you're offering next year on coastal erosion.
Dr. Peters	OK.
Amanda	First, I wanted to know which country the course focuses on.

Dr. Peters   Well, I don't restrict myself. As we're in Australia, it's natural that I spend quite a bit of the course focusing on the coastline here. Australia has a coastline of nearly thirty-six thousand kilometres and around <u>fifty per cent **(Q21)**</u> of that is made up of sand. Australia provides us with so much material to work on and is currently such a topical subject that we don't need to study anywhere else. That would make the course a little limited though and so we look at various other places around the world.

Amanda   What are some of the other locations?

Dr. Peters   There are some <u>cliff formations **(Q22)**</u> in California that are in danger from the Pacific there, so we look at that. A lot of the countries in Western Africa have erosion problems and this is quite an important part of the course.

Amanda   Is it true that the West African erosion problem is because of human activities?

Dr. Peters   It's simplistic to blame problems on only one cause, but human actions are certainly part of the problem. The removal of sand and gravel from the coast to use for construction and human coastal constructions, such as ports, harbours and jetties, with the associated dredging required for ships to approach, have all exacerbated the problems. Natural phenomena, such as wave actions, tide, sea currents and winds also play a role, although it's argued <u>global warming **(Q23)**</u> affects these as well.

Amanda   Are there any other places we study?

Dr. Peters   We look at some severe erosion areas around the world, so we can study the causes, consequences and action taken in these areas. This includes some locations in the UK, Louisiana and Hawaii. There are various others as well.

Amanda   Do we have many field trips?

Dr. Peters   Yes, we do, but only in Australia and to places not too far away. We can't afford to go to Africa and California unfortunately! Our main trip is a study of the Gold Coast and we visit a number of <u>hotspots **(Q24)**</u> on the coast there.

Amanda   What will we do on the field trips?

Dr. Peters   A lot of survey work and research. Fortunately, we have the figures of previous students available, so we have great data on past erosion measurements. You'll have access to all these data and then you'll need to do your own measurements.

Amanda   How long will the trips be?

Dr. Peters   They'll be mostly day trips when possible to keep costs down. That will of course be locations that are fairly close to us here. There will also have to be some <u>overnight **(Q25)**</u> trips. We get a lot of work done on these trips, but it's a lot of fun as well.

You now have some time to look at questions twenty-six to thirty.

(20 second gap)

Now listen to the rest of the discussion and answer questions twenty-six to thirty.

Amanda   Can I ask you a little about assessment?

Dr. Peters   Yes, of course. The assessment is divided between essays, a project and one exam at the end of the academic year.

Amanda   What does each of those entail?

Dr. Peters   You'll have six essays. These will be set on different areas of the course and they will try to make you look more deeply at different geographical locations and at the different causes and consequences **(Q26)** of the problems and actions taken or planned. The project is for you to choose an area of study that has interested you. As we're in Australia, it's natural that most students choose an erosion issue or situation here, as information is more readily available and the locations are easier to visit. We do have students who choose overseas locations, particularly foreign students **(Q27)**, of course.

Amanda   And the exam?

Dr. Peters   The exam is two hours **(Q28)** in length and will assess the whole course. Any part of the course can come up and students will be expected to have a good working knowledge of the various aspects of the different things that they studied.

Amanda   How are the assessments weighted?

Dr. Peters   The exam is fifteen per cent of the final course grade and the essays are thirty-five per cent. The project makes up the other fifty per cent.

Amanda   What happens if students fail?

Dr. Peters   The exam **(Q29)** can be re-taken if the students fail, but the essays and project cannot be done again. It's not that easy a course. There is a lot of knowledge to acquire and synthesise.

Amanda   Do you get many students who fail?

Dr. Peters   No, not really. The key thing for us is the student selection. We try and make sure that we choose able and motivated students. We check qualifications very carefully to ensure that all students have the necessary background and skills to cope with what the course demands.

Amanda   That sounds reassuring.

Dr. Peters   I hope so. Of course there are occasionally some problems, but usually, the course tutors **(Q30)** can see fairly early by the essay performances if any students are struggling and they try to intervene and help before the problem students' situations become irretrievable.

Amanda   Well, thanks, Dr. Peters. That was really helpful!

Dr. Peters   You're welcome, Amanda. Goodbye.

Amanda   Goodbye.

That is the end of part three. You will now have half a minute to check your answers.

(30 second gap)

Now turn to part four.

Part four. You will hear part of a biology lecture on the emperor penguin. First you have some time to look at questions thirty-one to forty.

(50 second gap)

Now listen carefully and answer questions thirty-one to forty.

Good morning and welcome to this lecture on the emperor penguin. Penguins in general are flightless birds perfectly designed for the marine environment. They are excellent swimmers with a torpedo shaped body, feet and tail that act as a rudder and flippers that act as propellers. A waterproof coat of feathers with an under-layer of woolly down plus a fat **(Q31)** layer protects them against the cold.

Penguins eat mainly small fish and krill. In turn, penguins become food for other marine animals, namely leopard seals and killer whales **(Q32)**. On land, their main predators are skuas and sheathbills, which are both carnivorous birds that take both eggs and chicks.

There is still debate about the classification of some penguins, and depending on which authority is followed, there are seventeen, and perhaps up to twenty, species of penguin. Four of these species live and nest on and around the Antarctic continent and the rest are found in sub-Antarctic regions.

The largest of the penguin species, the emperor grows up to 1.15 metres tall and weighs up to forty kilograms. They are very deep divers, often diving to about two hundred and fifty metres with dives lasting on average three to six minutes. Their menu is varied and includes fish, krill and squid.

A truly hardy animal, the emperor penguin is the only warm-blooded animal that breeds during the Antarctic winter, surviving blizzards, darkness and wind chill equivalent to temperatures as low as minus sixty degrees Celsius. Every year around late March, adult emperor penguins leave the pack ice and may walk up to two hundred kilometres over its frozen surface to their breeding sites. They require stable, long-lasting fast ice **(Q33)** on which to breed. In May or June, the females lay one egg and then make the long walk back to open water, eating again for the first time in about two months. In the meantime, the egg is kept on the feet of the father, protected under the layers of feathers and fat of its abdomen **(Q34)**. During the next two months, the father fasts while keeping watch until its chick hatches. Miraculously, at that time, the mother returns with food. By that time of year, July - August, food can then be obtained more easily, because adjacent ocean areas have been swept free of sea ice by strong winds.

Two of the most northern emperor penguin populations are located at Pointe Géologie, Adélie Land, and Dion Island located on the northwestern Antarctic Peninsula. In this warmer part of Antarctica, both emperor penguin populations have declined over recent decades. At Pointe Géologie, the population has declined by about fifty per cent over the past fifty years. High mortality occurred during the late 1970's, the cause of which is not yet known, and the population has not recovered since **(Q35)**. The decrease in the Dion Island colony was brought about by large-scale disappearance of sea ice in that region.

The emperor penguins' main predator is the leopard seal. The leopard seal lives in the ocean and waits until some emperor penguins enter the water and then eats the weakest one. Also some birds eat the eggs and the chicks when they are about a month old. Furthermore, emperor penguins face threats from overfishing and rising temperatures. The <u>overfishing</u> **(Q36)** is killing most of the emperor penguins' food source.

Climate change has caused profound changes in the Antarctic ecosystem and impacts the emperor penguins in diverse ways, such as causing ice shelves to collapse and icebergs to calve. A recent report claims that under <u>two degrees Celsius</u> **(Q37)** global warming will lead to a decrease in sea ice thickness and an increase in open water area. This will severely challenge around forty percent of the emperor penguin population in terms of finding satisfactory <u>nesting areas</u> **(Q38)**. The report goes on to say that because of this, emperor penguins will lose twenty per cent of their number in the next ten years; the report also calls for emperor penguins to be put on the endangered animals list. Global warming can paradoxically cause more and less ice at different times of year. Too much ice can mean that the female has much further to travel to begin to feed following the birth and much further therefore to return to bring the food to the hatched chick and waiting father. Too little ice can mean that <u>breeding platforms</u> **(Q39)** can be scarcer or break up earlier before the chicks are ready. The report hopes that emperor penguins may adapt to the changing conditions, by climbing onto land or higher, safer ice, but at this point, this is only conjecture.

A final threat is that the king penguin may also easily displace the emperor penguin because of its extended breeding season, which allows it to exist in areas with lower <u>food</u> **(Q40)** availability.

That is the end of part four. You will now have half a minute to check your answers.

(30 second gap)

That is the end of listening test one.

LISTENING TEST 2 TRANSCRIPT

This recording is copyright by Robert Nicholson and Simone Braverman, all rights reserved.

IELTS listening practice tests. Test two. In the IELTS test you hear some recordings and you have to answer questions on them. You have time to read the instructions and questions and check your work. All recordings are played only once. The test is in four parts. Now turn to part one.

Part one. You will hear a conversation between a man and a woman discussing a celebration at an outdoor centre.

First you have some time to look at questions one to five.

(20 second gap)

Now we begin. You should answer the questions as you listen, as the recording is not played twice. Listen carefully to the conversation and answer questions one to five.

John   Good morning. Welcome to John's Outdoor Centre.

Katherine   Thank you.

John   What can I do for you?

Katherine   I'm looking for a suitable place to celebrate my birthday. When I drove by this place a couple of days ago, I thought that this might be a good place, as it is quite far from the city. It would be a really different place to be.

John   May I ask when your birthday is?

Katherine   On the eighteenth of <u>May</u> **(Q1)**.

John   Alright. In the summer. That's a very nice time. We would be able to use the stone oven, make a bonfire and use the camping area if you wish to stay for the night.

Katherine   That sounds great!

John   OK. May I first take your phone number and full name before we start to talk about any further details?

Katherine   Of course! My full name is Katherine Truman – that's spelt K - A - T - H - E - R - I - N - E and <u>T - R - U - M - A - N</u> **(Q2)**. And my telephone number is oh three four eight, two three seven, eight five five.

John   Got that, thank you. So, when's the party supposed to be?

Katherine   I'd like to celebrate on the twentieth of May and the party should start at <u>6 p.m.</u> **(Q3)**, because I still need to work on that day and then get ready for the party, which I guess you know will take some time!

John   Oh dear, working on a Saturday. I know nobody who enjoys that! Well, my calendar shows that the date is free and, up to now, there haven't been any other bookings made for that day yet. However, horse riding **(Q4)** is not available on that day, as the horses will be resting. I hope that you didn't plan to do that?

Katherine   Oh no, that's fine. I think that food and a bonfire will be fine for my guests.

John   Speaking of guests. How many people have you invited or are you intending to invite?

Katherine   It'll be thirty people **(Q5)**.

John   Okay.

Before the conversation continues, you have some time to look at questions six to ten.

(20 second gap)

Now listen carefully and answer questions six to ten.

Katherine   Before I book any activities for the party, I would like to have a list of the activities that are available and their prices. My budget is eight hundred dollars and I would like to stay within this boundary. This must also include the food and drinks consumed.

John   Okay. Let's go through the price lists. So, as you can see, we are open from seven a.m. to eight p.m. from Monday through Friday. On the weekends, however, we are open from eight-thirty a.m. to seven p.m **(Q6)**. These opening times don't interfere with your party, as you're planning to spend the night here, aren't you?

Katherine   It depends on the price I would have to pay.

John   Okay, so we offer various activities. To start with, we can offer to make a bonfire for fifteen dollars. This money is just to pay for the wood we need.

Katherine   Yeah, that sounds great. I'll definitely book the bonfire. What else is there?

John   There are also various tours we offer, like for instance the boat tour, which takes between two and three hours and costs six dollars **(Q7)** per person. Then there is the cycling tour for eight dollars per person and the hiking tour for twenty-five dollars per person. Our special offer for the summer is baking in our newly built stone oven. This can be done in groups of up to fifteen people maximum and costs five dollars **(Q8)** per person.

Katherine   Okay, that sounds great. Let me see. I would really like to bake, so I'll take that. And I'll also take the boat tour.

John   Alright. Let's get to the food and drinks. We offer a small and a large buffet. The small one serves approximately forty people and costs two hundred dollars, while the large one costs <u>four hundred dollars</u> **(Q9)** and serves eighty to a hundred people. As an extra, you can also book a lamb on a spit for thirty-five dollars. I think for you, I'd plan one hundred and fifty dollars for the drinks.

Katherine   Alright, then I'll take the small buffet please and the drinks of course.

John   Okay, and lastly we offer three types of accommodation. We can offer camping with tents for forty dollars per tent and they hold four people each. We also have some tipis, which are big tents that hold up to twenty people, for eighty dollars per tipi. However, our greatest attraction is the tree house for <u>a hundred dollars</u> **(Q10)**. It can house up to twenty people as well.

Katherine   Okay. Half of my guests will drive back home, so the tree house will be perfect. Great! According to my calculations that makes seven hundred and ninety-five dollars in total, so that's just under my budget.

John   Yes, I think that's right.

Katherine   Okay. Thank you for that. Could we take a look at the tree house?

John   Of course we can. It's right over there.

That is the end of part one. You will now have half a minute to check your answers.

(30 second gap)

Now turn to part two.

Part two. You will hear a woman giving some people information about a walking tour around the town of Barton. First you have some time to look at questions eleven to fourteen.

(20 second gap)

Now listen carefully to the information talk and answer questions eleven to fourteen.

Good morning, everyone. My name's Sharon. Thanks for coming today to my walking tour of the town of Barton. First, I'd like to give you a quick overview of where we're going to today.

Right now, we're in front of the Barton Tourist Office. From here, we'll move down the pedestrian road towards the river. While we're on this road, <u>we'll first pass the Town Hall on the right and then right after that, the old town prison. Opposite the prison we'll see the town museum</u> **(Q11)**, although we won't be visiting that this morning. When we get to the river, you'll see the river docks, where people can take boat trips up and down the River Stroud. We'll turn right here and walk down the path next to the river. While we're walking, we'll first see on the right the Museum of Modern Art and then after that, the oldest house in the town and then, just before we get to Charlton Bridge, the memorial to Sir John Barton, the founder of the town. <u>Across the river from the Modern Art Museum, we'll see the impressive facade of the main town mosque</u> **(Q12)**, which was built only fifteen years ago for the Muslim population of the town.

We won't cross Charlton Bridge, but <u>we'll go to the right again and walk up the street, stopping at Regent Square, in the centre of which is the town's war memorial fountain</u> **(Q13)**. There's a great ice cream parlour there and we can rest a while, look at the view and eat some ice cream. When we're done with that, we'll take the road that goes right off the square and walk back down towards the Tourist Office again. <u>While we're walking, you'll see Barton Shopping Mall on the right</u> **(Q14)**. We won't stop there on our tour, but if you want to do some shopping, it's only a short walk back. There are a number of interesting things to see on the left. You'll first see the town's famous gothic church and then the library and sports centre. For your information, the town's train station is right behind the library as we pass it and the cinema is next to that.

You now have some time to look at questions fifteen to twenty.

(20 second gap)

Now listen to the rest of the information talk and answer questions fifteen to twenty.

I'll be speaking at each of the attractions to let you know all the interesting information, so I think the tour will take around <u>two and a half hours</u> **(Q15)** and that's including the twenty-minute break for ice cream. This afternoon, I'll be doing a three-hour walking tour of the town museum that we will pass early on in this walk.

By the way, <u>I do not charge anything for this walk</u> **(Q16)** and I live only by tips. If you feel the walk has been worthwhile, past walkers with me have tipped between five and twenty pounds. It depends on your budget and how good a job you think I've done.

Now, just before we begin, I've been asked to talk a little bit about the entertainment on offer tonight around the town.

Tonight is a weekday, so there's not much in the way of live music, which someone asked me about. Nor will you find here much in the way of football, as the town team only plays at the weekends. <u>At the town cinema, there is a double bill film with films on novels by the famous Russian novelist</u> **(Q17-Q20)**, Leo Tolstoy. That starts at seven o'clock. <u>We won't see the town theatre on our walk today, but there is a tour of it offered tonight as there are no performances tonight</u> **(Q17-Q20)**. You might be tired of tours today by then though!

<u>One fun thing to do that does not involve any walking is at the pub called The Crown. They have their weekly quiz on tonight</u> **(Q17-Q20)**. I often go to that myself with some friends. <u>What I will be doing tonight though is to go to a cafe in the town's main square, where I will be watching some street theatre</u> **(Q17-Q20)** that is scheduled this evening to start at eight o'clock. Barton is quite well known for this, so it would be an excellent and different thing to do. There is some tennis on in London too and I told some people that they could watch that on TV in their hotel or in pubs, but I've been told that bad weather in London has stopped all play, so that won't be an option any more.

So, those are a few things you could consider and maybe I'll see you later if you do what I'm doing. Now, let's get on with our walking tour!

That is the end of part two. You will now have half a minute to check your answers.

(30 second gap)

Now turn to part three.

Part three. You will hear three students and a lecturer discussing the students' agriculture projects. First you have some time to look at questions twenty-one to twenty-five.

(20 second gap)

Now listen carefully and answer questions twenty-one to twenty-five.

Professor Evans   Now, you three have come to tell me how you're getting on with your agriculture projects.

Simona   That's right, Professor Evans.

Professor Evans: So, to start with, I'd like to you to tell me about the collection of your primary data. Would you like to start, Steve?

Steve   Of course. I've been studying how parasites affect the growing of potatoes in this part of the world. In order to gather data, I've liaised with some farmers **(Q21)** local to the university and they've nearly all allowed me to work in their fields and collect data. The problem is that all the farmers around here use insecticides that kill the parasites. It's been easy therefore to collect information on farms with no parasite dangers, but it was a challenge to get information on farms that had parasites.

Professor Evans   How did you manage to get the parasite data then?

Steve   I had to rent a field **(Q22)** away from other farms and plant potatoes myself. I of course did not use insecticides and I've managed to collect enough data to compare with the other data on farms with insecticides.

Robert   Wasn't that expensive, Steve?

Steve   Not too bad actually. There was an initial outlay for the rental and the planting, but I managed to do a deal with a local farmer, who harvested and sold them. He paid me for them and, as they were bio-potatoes with no insecticides, I got a good price and I even made a small profit. My housemates and I also ate potatoes every day for a couple of weeks!

Professor Evans   How about you, Simona?

Simona   Well, as you know, I'm doing a project on growth rates **(Q23)** in different varieties of tomatoes. Now the weather here is not so good for tomatoes, but the university botanical garden assigned me an area in one of their greenhouses and so I was able to grow plenty of varieties and I had lots of success with gathering data for my project. Like Steve, my house ate lots of tomatoes through the early summer!

Professor Evans   So, Robert. How did you get on?

Robert   I had a lot of initial problems. I wanted to look at different soils and how acidity **(Q24)** affected growth of certain plants. I started a bit too late and I wasn't able to get agreements with different places about being able to use the different bits of land with the acidities that I wanted.

Professor Evans   How did you deal with that?

Robert   In the end, I just had to ditch that idea and go for my plan B. This was about the growing techniques of apple farmers. The season **(Q25)** starts later, so I had enough time to prepare and contact farmers. Where I live at home with my parents is an important apple-growing area, so I was able to use my holidays to gather all the information there.

You now have some time to look at questions twenty-six to thirty.

(20 second gap)

Now listen to the rest of the discussion and answer questions twenty-six to thirty.

Professor Evans   So, do you have any questions about the rest of the work that you need to do on the project?

Steve   We're a little confused about when we need to be finished by. We've heard different things.

Professor Evans   You need to give me a hard copy **(Q26)** by the twenty-eighth of February next year. I then have a week to read your projects and make comments on what you need to do to improve. You then have until the thirtieth of April **(Q27)** to submit the final version to the university. Remember as well that you can't give in a hard copy this year. It has to be submitted by email to the course administrator, which is Mrs. Roberts. Her email address is in the course literature, on our website and on the department noticeboard.

Simona   There is no mention in the project guide about a word limit. Is there one?

Professor Evans   Yes, there is. It's in the project guide, but it's hard to find. We'll make it clearer next year. Last year, the word limit was deemed insufficient at eight thousand words, so this year it's been increased by two thousand **(Q28)**. We hope that this will give you all the scope to do a good job. Be careful not to waffle though or we'll be cutting it down by a thousand next year for those after you. The limit also doesn't include the appendices **(Q29)**, which is another change from last year. There's no limit on them, but please be sensible and don't give me twenty thousand words!

Robert   I've a last question, Professor. What happens if our projects are not good enough?

Professor Evans   That doesn't happen very often, Robert. I'll get to read the first drafts and, unless the project is incredibly bad, I can give you the advice needed to get it up to scratch. If in the end it really does fail, then you won't be able to graduate **(Q30)**. You'd have to redo the project or do a different one the next year in your own time.

Robert   Thanks, Professor.

That is the end of part three. You will now have half a minute to check your answers.

(30 second gap)

Now turn to part four.

Part four. You will hear part of a psychology lecture on the Rorschach Test. First you have some time to look at questions thirty-one to forty.

(50 second gap)

Now listen carefully and answer questions thirty-one to forty.

Good afternoon, everyone. Today, we continue our overview of the different psychological tests that have been used over the years in order to profile people and to explain out-of-the ordinary behaviour. The test we'll look at today is the Rorschach Test.

The Rorschach Test is a projective psychological test developed in nineteen twenty-one to measure thought disorder. It was first developed from the observation that schizophrenia patients often interpret ambiguous images in very unusual ways **(Q31)**. In the test, a participant is shown a series of ten ink blot cards and is directed to respond to each by saying what the ink blots look like. The Rorschach Test is practically the only test that evaluates in this way **(Q32)**.

The Rorschach ink blots are supposed to remain secret so as not to pollute the test population **(Q33)**. The theory behind the test, created by Hermann Rorschach, is that a test taker's spontaneous or unrehearsed responses reveal deep secrets or significant information about his or her personality or innermost thoughts. These days, nearly all psychologists avoid using the method applied to the Rorschach, as it is regarded as unreliable at best and dangerously misleading at worst **(Q34)**. A few psychologists, however, still believe in it as a valid diagnostic tool, despite the availability of more modern and sophisticated personality tests. The psychologists who do still see value in the Rorschach Test frequently argue amongst themselves as to the manner of its interpretation, the meaning of the results, and even its validity **(Q35)**. Several different schools of thought have even sprung up for the interpretation of the results, muddying the waters even further.

For those still using the Rorschach Test, the Exner Comprehensive System is one of the more popular scoring methodologies in use today. Based on the work of John E. Exner, responses are scored using a number of categories. There is a reference to the level of vagueness of the answer or if there is a synthesis of multiple images in the blot. What makes a subject say what he or she does is also significant. For example, how the respondents explain how the ink blots resemble what they think it resembles is very significant. Amongst other criteria, the degree of mental organising activity that is involved in producing the response and any illogical, incongruous, or incoherent aspects of responses are also used in evaluation. Using the scores for these categories, the examiner then performs a series of mathematical calculations producing a structural summary of the test data. The results of the structural summary are claimed to show personality characteristics **(Q36)** that have been demonstrated to be related to different kinds of responses. Both the calculations of scores and the interpretation are often done electronically.

The Rorschach Test is supposed to be administered in a very particular and rigid format in order to minimise variance **(Q37)** in the results. Like the cards themselves, the test procedure itself is also supposed to be kept secret from the general public. In the standard test protocol, test takers are given the cards one at a time in a specific order, and the psychologist is supposed to place them directly in the takers' hands facing up and in a particular orientation. The order is not supposed to vary. The genuine Rorschach cards are numbered on the back primarily for the psychologists' use. If takers notice the numbers or remark on them, a note is supposed to be made about this. The cards themselves are large, about seven by nine inches and are made of stiffened cardboard or, in modern variations, a textured plastic that mimics the feel of cardboard. Five of the cards have purely black and white images, two of the cards are black, white, and red, and the last three cards have various colours of ink used in the blots.

The test giver will almost never give any guidance **(Q38)**. They will instead tell the test takers that they're free to do whatever they like with the card. About fifty per cent of people who take the test flip or rotate the cards. It's reported that some psychologists will penalise people in terms of the results if they don't turn the cards around or upside-down!

During the test the psychologist or psychiatrist will record everything the taker says. In general, questioning or asking about the results are supposed to have significance to the test provider, as does asking nearly anything about the blots themselves. It used to be that the notes were taken in a special shorthand **(Q39)** that was specifically developed for the Rorschach Test, although these days many psychologists rely more on recordings and will only make cursory hand-written notes during the test. Often the psychologist will attempt to shield his or her note-taking from the takers so as not to distract them or make them nervous **(Q40)**, as this would create a skew in the test results.

That is the end of part four. You will now have half a minute to check your answers.

(30 second gap)

That is the end of listening test two.

LISTENING TEST 3 TRANSCRIPT

This recording is copyright by Robert Nicholson and Simone Braverman, all rights reserved.

IELTS listening practice tests. Test three. In the IELTS test you hear some recordings and you have to answer questions on them. You have time to read the instructions and questions and check your work. All recordings are played only once. The test is in four parts. Now turn to part one.

Part one. You will hear a conversation between a man and a woman discussing a mobile phone contract.

First you have some time to look at questions one to five.

(20 second gap)

Now we begin. You should answer the questions as you listen, as the recording is not played twice. Listen carefully to the conversation and answer questions one to five.

Tom	Hello. Welcome to R and N Mobile. My name's Tom. How can I help you?
Jennifer	Hello. I'd like to discuss my new mobile contract.
Tom	Would you mind giving me your customer ID?
Jennifer	Just a moment, please. Here it is. TR three four nine five seven three.
Tom	Thank you. Now, just for confirmation, could you provide me with your date of birth?
Jennifer	Sure. It's the twelfth of March, <u>nineteen eighty-two</u> **(Q1)**.
Tom	And what's the zip code of your current address?
Jennifer	It's eight five eight two three.
Tom	What's the number of your house at that location?
Jennifer	<u>Thirty</u> **(Q2)**.
Tom	And finally, your name, please?
Jennifer	Jennifer Wright.
Tom	Would you spell that, please?
Jennifer	Jennifer is J - E - double N - I - F - E - R. Wright is <u>W - R - I - G - H - T</u> **(Q3)**.
Tom	That's interesting. We had you before as Jennifer with only one N. I'll just change that. Now, I notice here that we don't have a home number for you. That can be very useful for us in case you have a problem on your mobile and we can't phone you on it.

Page 169

Jennifer	My home number is oh one nine three four, <u>nine eight one **(Q4)**,</u> three four two.
Tom	Finally, can you just confirm for me how you pay your monthly bill?
Jennifer	I do that with <u>direct debit **(Q5)**</u>.
Tom	OK, Miss Wright. Thank you. That has confirmed your identity.

Before the conversation continues, you have some time to look at questions six to ten.

(20 second gap)

Now listen carefully and answer questions six to ten.

Jennifer	Last Wednesday, I ordered a new contract, but I only saw yesterday that the terms have changed.
Tom	Absolutely right.
Jennifer	Now, I wanted to know whether I am also eligible to have an additional <u>two gigabytes **(Q6)**</u> of Internet each month.
Tom	Just a moment, please. *(pause)* OK. I just looked into this, and I'm sorry to say that you're not eligible.
Jennifer	Could you do anything about it?
Tom	As a matter of fact, you are in luck. As you did not yet activate the <u>SIM card **(Q7)**</u>, we will be able to send you a new contract along with a new SIM card.
Jennifer	That would be great. Are there any extra costs?
Tom	No, there will be no extra costs for you. Furthermore, you will also be able to use our TFR Network, which is one of the fastest available.
Jennifer	That sounds great. And how about the terms and conditions? Will I be able to terminate the contract?
Tom	Absolutely. You'll be able to terminate the contract, but you must, however, terminate <u>thirty **(Q8)**</u> days in advance.
Jennifer	Sounds great. And the price of <u>forty-five **(Q9)**</u> dollars per month will stay the same?
Tom	Exactly. May I proceed to delete your current contract and start the new one?
Jennifer	Absolutely. Could I also order a new mobile telephone?
Tom	Yes, you will be able to do that on our website. I will send you an email with the <u>link **(Q10)**</u> to our online store. I have now also changed your contract. You'll be able to reauthorise your payment, so you'll just need to sign here, please. That's it. Can I help you in any other way?

Page 170

Jennifer	No, that's all. Thank you very much.
Tom	You're welcome. Have a great day.

That is the end of part one. You will now have half a minute to check your answers.

(30 second gap)

Now turn to part two.

Part two. You will hear a man giving some people information about a holiday park. First you have some time to look at questions eleven to fifteen.

(20 second gap)

Now listen carefully to the information talk and answer questions eleven to fifteen.

Good morning, everyone. I'm Mr. Jenkins. I'd like to welcome you all today to our holiday park. Now you've all just spent the first night in your rooms and I hope you had a restful night. What I'd like to do is to tell you a little bit about the holiday park and what we have on offer for you.

As you may be aware, right now we're at the central coffee bar in the holiday park's main building, which is known as the Johnson Building. This is a large building in the very centre of the park. The coffee bar here is open every day **(Q11-Q15)** from six a.m. until eight p.m. It serves coffees, teas and other infusions, along with a variety of cold drinks and hot and cold snacks. It does not serve proper meals. For that, you'll need to go to one of our other restaurants, such as our pizzeria, French bistro or Asian street café elsewhere in the park. More of that later. Also available in this building is the main reception **(Q11-Q15)**. If you have any questions about the park, just go there and speak to our receptionists. One exception to this is anything to do with money. If you need to pay any bills or enquire about any costs, you'll need to go the finance office, which is in a separate building two hundred metres down the drive towards the main entrance. The maintenance team are also based there, so go there if there's anything wrong in your rooms or if you see anything faulty in the park. Back to where we are now. On the second floor, you'll find the first aid centre **(Q11-Q15)**, which has a lovely view of the lake and our cinema, which can be seen at the far end of the lake. There, we show old and new movies that hopefully appeal to all ages and tastes. The first aid centre has a nurse on duty twenty-four hours a day. The nurse can also get you to the doctor's surgery around half an hour away if there is anything she can't deal with. The rest of the second floor is taken up with various administration offices. On the floor above that is our Fitness Area **(Q11-Q15)**, which you can use at any time if you're over eighteen years of age. The Fitness Area does not include our saunas, steam rooms and treatment areas, which are found next to the main swimming pool. In the Fitness Area, you can work out on your own or book a session with one of our instructors. If you're feeling lazy, just go to our Internet café, which is next to the Fitness Area **(Q11-Q15)**. You can comfortably surf the net with a hot chocolate while watching the more motivated people work out!

You now have some time to look at questions sixteen to twenty.

(20 second gap)

Now listen to the rest of the information talk and answer questions sixteen to twenty.

We have plenty of activities for you and your family to enjoy. I'll describe some of these now.

In the south of the park is our water park complex. It's a ten-pound entrance fee for the public, but free for residents. Also, this area is open to the public in the afternoons, but in the mornings, it's reserved for the residents **(Q16)** of the holiday park and that's you. The water park opens from nine in the morning and closes at six in the late afternoon. The resident-only time changes at midday.

We also have a mini-golf, which is open from nine a.m. to six p.m. You don't need to own any equipment. Just turn up and we'll supply everything. The mini-golf can be quite busy, so we limit the number of people on the area at any one time. Groups of maximum five people are allowed to start playing at five-minute **(Q17)** intervals. Reservations are not permitted, so it's run on a first come, first play basis. There's no cost for the mini-golf.

For the keep-fit amongst you, we run a jogging club, which meets twice a day. The first session is at eight a.m. and covers a distance of around four **(Q18)** kilometres. The jog goes through the forest on easy flat trails. The second session is at five p.m. and is longer, at six kilometres. This also goes through the forest on well-tended trails, but is hillier and more demanding. Both the jogs are led by two of our fitness instructors. One will lead the jog and the other will bring up the rear. The sessions start with some warming-up exercises **(Q19)** and end with stretching.

Not far away is the historic town of Levington. With its medieval castle and the historic old town with the old fortified walls still standing, this is a popular visiting place for our guests. We have a minibus service that goes to Levington every day at one p.m. and returns at five p.m. There's an extra cost of two pounds return for this service. Tickets can be bought at the main reception area. You can also buy tickets from the bus driver **(Q20)**, but if all the tickets are sold, you may find yourself disappointed, so book ahead if you really want to go.

Before I carry on, are there any questions so far?

That is the end of part two. You will now have half a minute to check your answers.

 (30 second gap)

Now turn to part three.

Part three. You will hear a student giving his presentation and interacting with his university teacher. First you have some time to look at questions twenty-one to twenty-five.

(20 second gap)

Now listen carefully and answer questions twenty-one to twenty-five.

Alex   Good morning, Professor Norris. We're all here now.

Professor Norris Thanks, Alex. Good morning everyone. Today, we're going to hear from Alex, who is going to do his presentation. First of all, I'd like to tell you that <u>next week's seminar on your next essay</u> <u>(Q21)</u> is not in this room, but in room four two five in the history department. It's the room that has all the pictures of the Great Wall of China in it. We're doing a swap with the history department for just that day, so that they can use this larger room, which will suit their purposes. Now, Alex. Are you ready?

Alex Yes, thank you, Professor Norris. I'm ready.

Professor Norris So, what do you plan to talk about today?

Alex Well, many of you will have heard of the Forest of Dean.

Professor Norris Let everyone know where it is, just in case.

Alex It's on the borders of south Wales and England, near the River Severn, which is the longest river in the UK.

Professor Norris Thank you. Now, what are you going to tell us about the Forest of Dean?

Alex I'd like to focus today on the new colonies of wild boar that have sprung up in the forest. These are wild pigs, if you didn't know. <u>This fits in with our course subject, which explores how new non-indigenous species can affect a natural environment</u> <u>(Q22)</u>.

Professor Norris Surely wild boars are native to the UK though?

Alex They were, but they went extinct here around seven hundred years ago. I know it's not quite the same, but seven hundred years is a long time and the forest environment adapted to the boars' absence. It's pretty much the same as if a foreign species were introduced.

Professor Norris Yes. I think I agree with that.

Alex So, boars were once common in the Forest of Dean and were hunted for food. In medieval times, boars from the royal forest were supplied for the King's table. There is a record of an order for a hundred boars and sows for a Christmas feast in twelve fifty-four. <u>Boars are thought to have become extinct in Britain due to over-hunting not long after this time, although disease also was a more minor factor</u> <u>(Q23)</u>. The farming of wild boars in Britain became fashionable in the nineteen seventies, but <u>the principal issue facing the industry was that it was not particularly profitable</u> <u>(Q24)</u>. In nineteen ninety-nine, boars escaped, or were released, from a farm near the Forest of Dean. In two thousand and four, a group of about sixty farm-raised boars were dumped near the forest.

Professor Norris Really! So many boar escaped from one farm!

Alex No. In the second case, the boar were released. A farm was going out of business and it was easier for them to just release the boar rather than go through the selling process.

Professor Norris Were they prosecuted?

Alex I'm afraid I don't know. I just focused on the boars.

Professor Norris That's OK. It's not important.

Page 173

Anyway, very soon it was clear that the two released populations had merged and, in spite of ...es by the Forestry Commission regarding limited bloodlines, a healthy breeding population was surviving in the forest. <u>The breeding has caused the population to grow steadily and there is now believed to be in excess of eight hundred boars in the Forest of Dean</u> **(Q25)**, with the population expanding out into neighbouring areas. Boar are now feral throughout the forest area and the Forest of Dean population is the largest of the breeding populations that now exist in England.

You now have some time to look at questions twenty-six to thirty.

(20 second gap)

Now listen to the rest of the presentation and answer questions twenty-six to thirty.

Alex   The problem with the released and breeding wild boars in the Forest of Dean is that the population is getting too large.

Professor Norris   Who is actually responsible for controlling the population?

Alex   That's an interesting legal point. Once the animals escaped, the government's position is that free roaming wild boars are feral wild animals and as such do not belong to anyone, and that responsibility for managing wild boars rests with the <u>land owner</u> **(Q26)**. Thus, feral wild boars have the status of a wild animal, such as wild deer, and foxes.

Professor Norris   What will happen to the excess numbers then?

Alex   Well, many people feel that the numbers are not a problem. Although there are stories of wild boars being dangerous, locals next to the Forest of Dean say this is not the case. When wild boars are disturbed by walkers, the tendency is for one of the larger sows to position themselves between the walkers and the young, often accompanied by much snorting, whilst the <u>family group</u> **(Q27)** leads the young to safety. Once the family has moved off, the defending sow will usually suddenly turn and run off to rejoin the group. The defending sow may well also be provoked into a mock charge at the intruding people, particularly if that group continue to approach for a better look, or simply because they have not noticed the boars. Male boars can be more aggressive, but so far there are only stories of dogs being chased.

Professor Norris   I don't expect that the government have accepted the stories of locals!

Alex   Absolutely not. There are now regular culls of the wild boar population by the Forestry Commission in the Forest of Dean. <u>Forest rangers</u> **(Q28)** on specific days go out and destroy carefully selected numbers of the animals. The problem is that animal rights activists object to the culls and try to disrupt them.

Professor Norris   Can't the forest just be closed on cull days?

Alex   No, the forest is open land. The activists know that the forest rangers conducting the cull have to stay close to big paths, so that they can bring vehicles to move the dead carcasses of the animals away. The activists just divide the forest up and watch over the <u>big paths</u> **(Q29)** and make lots of noise and move bait.

Professor Norris   Are the activists successful?

Page 174

Alex   To a certain extent, yes. It's a big forest and they can't be everywhere, but they create enough disruption that they have spoiled quite a few of the planned cull days. The forests rangers are quite annoyed about this and point out that the large numbers of wild boar can affect the lives of other inhabitants of the forest. The forest rangers haven't given up though and they now keep the cull dates secret **(Q30)** and try and catch the activists unprepared.

That is the end of part three. You will now have half a minute to check your answers.

(30 second gap)

Now turn to part four.

Part four. You will hear part of an environmental science lecture on bottom trawling fishing in New Zealand. First you have some time to look at questions thirty-one to forty.

(50 second gap)

Now listen carefully and answer questions thirty-one to forty.

Good morning. Today in this environmental sciences lecture, we are going to look at bottom trawling, and we will focus this time on our own waters here in New Zealand.

The area of ocean and seabed out to two hundred nautical miles from New Zealand's coastline is called the exclusive economic zone, or EEZ. This area covers approximately three point nine million square kilometres and is the fifth largest EEZ in the world. The depth of the sea within this area can extend to ten thousand **(Q31)** metres. The marine landscapes within New Zealand's EEZ include spectacular underwater mountains, valleys, geysers, and muddy flats. These are home to corals, sponges, and other unique forms of marine life.

Fishing can damage the seabed and the corals, sponges and other life found there, particularly when bottom-trawl or dredge fishing gear is used. How much damage occurs depends on a number of factors, including the type of seabed habitat that is being fished and the particular equipment **(Q32)** being used.

Conservation groups say bottom-trawling is the most destructive type of fishing undertaken in the world's oceans today. Bottom trawling involves dragging huge, heavy nets along the sea floor. Large metal plates and rubber wheels attached to these nets move along the bottom and crush nearly everything in their path. The bottom trawling net indiscriminately catches every life and object it encounters. Thus, many creatures end up mistakenly caught and thrown overboard dead or dying, including endangered fish and even vulnerable deep-sea corals, which can live for several hundred years. This collateral damage, which is known as the by-catch **(Q33)**, can amount to ninety percent of a trawl's total catch. Conservationists claim that all evidence indicates that deep-water life forms are very slow to recover from such damage, taking decades to hundreds of years, if they recover at all. Commercial fishing companies **(Q34)**, not surprisingly, tell a different story.

All human activity has some degree of impact on the natural environment. What is important is that these activities are closely monitored to ensure that impacts are managed and kept to an acceptable level. The New Zealand Ministry of Fisheries says it closely monitors bottom trawling as part of a comprehensive fisheries management regime. In New Zealand, one of the ways this is achieved on land is by setting aside large areas as national parks, where activities such as intensive farming are not permitted. In the marine environment, the approach is no different **(Q35)**. In 2007, the New Zealand Government, with the support of the fishing industry, closed one point one million square kilometres of seabed to bottom trawling and dredging, which is close to a third of New Zealand's entire EEZ. The seventeen separate closed areas, known as benthic protection areas, or BPA's, mainly cover areas of New Zealand waters that have never been trawled **(Q36)**. The seabed within these areas is largely in an untouched state and includes the full range of deep-sea underwater landscapes that occur across the EEZ. In addition to the BPA's, eighteen areas around underwater seamounts and geysers have been closed to all types of trawling, because of the unique marine life that is found there. Across New Zealand's EEZ, half of all known seamounts and all known active hydrothermal vents are closed to all trawling **(Q37)**.

In addition to the BPA's, the New Zealand Ministry of Fisheries says most of the New Zealand EEZ is deeper than one thousand two hundred and fifty metres and there is very little bottom trawling below that depth in New Zealand. Scientists have recently calculated that in excess of ninety-one per cent **(Q38)** of the New Zealand EEZ has never been bottom trawled. Finally, the New Zealand Ministry of Fisheries says it also regularly monitors where fishing vessels have operated, and the type and quantity of marine species, such as corals and sponges, which are caught.

New Zealand claims it is a world leader in successfully managing the effects that bottom trawling has on the seabed, closing one of the largest areas of marine space to bottom trawling in the world. Conservation groups are not happy with the New Zealand government though. They say that the ban doesn't extend to all vulnerable ecosystems **(Q39)**, and that some of the areas covered have already been fished out or are too deep to bottom trawl anyway. Of course, one third protection that the New Zealand government is so proud of leaves the two thirds unprotected and even if one third of a particular environment is protected, the damage inflicted in the other two thirds does have an impact on the rest. Conservation groups say that the only real way to protect the seabeds is to ban bottom trawling altogether and that if this means that consumers have to pay more for their fish, then this is a reasonable price to pay to preserve the underwater environment surrounding New Zealand. A final less noticed effect, but extremely important none the less, is that small community economies **(Q40)** are affected, as their fishermen's catch sizes are strongly affected by the enormous takes of industrial trawlers.

That is the end of part four. You will now have half a minute to check your answers.

(30 second gap)

That is the end of listening test three.

LISTENING TEST 4 TRANSCRIPT

This recording is copyright by Robert Nicholson and Simone Braverman, all rights reserved.

IELTS listening practice tests. Test four. In the IELTS test you hear some recordings and you have to answer questions on them. You have time to read the instructions and questions and check your work. All recordings are played only once. The test is in four parts. Now turn to part one.

Part one. You will hear a conversation between a man and a woman as the woman changes her family's hotel reservation.

First you have some time to look at questions one to five.

(20 second gap)

Now we begin. You should answer the questions as you listen, as the recording is not played twice. Listen carefully to the conversation and answer questions one to five.

Jake   The Sutherland Hotel. Jake speaking. How can I help you?

Mrs. Easton   Hello, my name is Mrs. Jane Easton. I have a reservation with you for next week, but I'd like to make a change.

Jake   OK. Do you have the reservation number with you?

Mrs. Easton   Yes. It's EZT four eight six, nine seven eight.

Jake   OK. I have your details here. I just need to take some details from you in order to confirm your identity. First of all, can you tell me your full name again?

Mrs. Easton   It's Mrs. Jane Easton. Easton is spelled <u>E - A - S - T - O - N</u> **(Q1)**.

Jake   And can I have your full address, including the postcode?

Mrs. Easton   It's <u>thirty</u> **(Q2)** Richmond Rise, Birkdale, Auckland. The postcode is oh six two six.

Jake   And can I have your date of birth, please?

Mrs. Easton   It's the fourteenth <u>October</u> **(Q3)** nineteen eighty-five.

Jake   Now, there's a couple of things missing from the reservation details. Can I ask you about them quickly, please?

Mrs. Easton   Yes, of course.

Jake   How did you find out about us?

Mrs. Easton   I found you in an Internet search.

Jake	What website did you use?

Mrs. Easton	It was <u>hotels.com</u> **(Q4)**. I always use this website when I'm looking for hotels.

Jake	Yes. We get a lot of bookings from that website.

Mrs. Easton	They're very good. I have never had a bad experience using them.

Jake	And do you know if the website charged you a <u>commission</u> **(Q5)** for getting you the booking with us?

Mrs. Easton	No. It was clear from the start that they only received that from you. I paid nothing to them.

Jake	Thanks very much.

Before the conversation continues, you have some time to look at questions six to ten.

(20 second gap)

Now listen carefully and answer questions six to ten.

Jake	That's lovely, Mrs. Easton. Now, what can I do for you? You said you needed to change your reservation. Let me know what needs to be done and I'll make the changes and confirm everything by email.

Mrs. Easton	Thank you. At present, I have a reservation for myself and my husband, Michael. We've decided that we're going to bring our children with us now.

Jake	That's no problem. Can you give me the details of them with their ages?

Mrs. Easton	There are two of them, both boys. Mark is <u>thirteen</u> **(Q6)** and Max is eight.

Jake	Would you like separate rooms for the boys?

Mrs. Easton	No, just one twin room is fine for them both.

Jake	Now, you and your husband have a sea view. Do you want that for your children's room? A sea view is more expensive, of course.

Mrs. Easton	No. We don't need a <u>sea view</u> **(Q7)** for them. They'll just be sleeping there.

Jake	Is there anything else?

Mrs. Easton	Yes, I need to change the dates. At present, we're coming on Friday the twenty-second of May. As we're bringing the children, we won't be able to get to you until the following day. We planned to stay until the following Wednesday and we won't change that.

Jake	So, I just need to add the extra room for the boys and take off one day from the start of the booking.

Mrs. Easton	That's right. Can you let me know the new price?

Jake   Let me look. You and your husbands' price is one day cheaper. For the boys, Mark gets charged the full rate, but Max gets the child rate. Your old price was one thousand two hundred dollars and the new one is <u>two thousand dollars **(Q8)**</u> exactly. That includes all the local and district taxes.

Mrs. Easton   Can I get a receipt for that?

Jake   I can't do that for you now, but of course you'll be issued one when at the hotel.

Mrs. Easton   I think that's everything, then.

Jake   OK, Mrs Peters. Let me just check everything. So, the booking is held with your VISA card with the last four numbers eight five three seven. Is that still alright?

Mrs. Easton   Yes. That's fine. Do I need to add to the <u>deposit **(Q9)**</u> I've paid?

Jake   No, what you've paid already is fine.

Mrs. Easton   Will the hotel know that I've paid it?

Jake   Oh yes. Don't worry about that. It's all in the system. Now, as I said earlier, I'll send you a confirmation by email. I have your address already in the system. Now, is there anything else?

Mrs. Easton   Actually, yes. I've just thought of something. Is <u>breakfast **(Q10)**</u> included for everyone?

Jake   Yes. You all get that included in the price. Anything else?

Mrs. Easton   No. I think that's everything. Thanks very much for your help.

Jake   You're welcome. Goodbye.

Mrs. Easton   Goodbye.

That is the end of part one. You will now have half a minute to check your answers.

(30 second gap)

Now turn to part two.

Part two. You will hear a man giving some people information about a tour of a chocolate factory. First you have some time to look at questions eleven to fifteen.

(20 second gap)

Now listen carefully to the information talk and answer questions eleven to fifteen.

Good morning, everyone. My name's Marcus and I've been asked to tell you a little about tours around our chocolate factory.

The chocolate factory has always been a family business and it was constructed in <u>1924</u> **(Q11)**. We found there was a demand for guided tours a few years ago, as our brand is so well known that people want to have a look at how we operate here.

The factory does not operate twenty-four hours a day. It has done in the past, but it's not needed right now. The factory employs <u>twenty-five</u> **(Q12)** people full time. This includes the operating and maintenance staff, who are responsible for making the chocolate, and the office staff, who are responsible for marketing, finance and all other aspects of our business.

I'll now tell you what you see when you come on a tour. We meet in the reception area of the administration area. Here you will be given some orientation, a visitor's badge and a sterile hair net that must be worn in the manufacturing area, so that we keep in line with our hygiene policy. There will also be a short safety talk by our <u>health and safety</u> **(Q13)** officer.

The tour starts with seeing where the raw chocolate arrives. We don't refine the raw material from the cacao bean. The raw chocolate is melted down in enormous vats. Depending on which product is being manufactured, different <u>ingredients</u> **(Q14)** are blended. These include milk, sugar, lecithin, which is an emulsifier, vanilla, cinnamon, fruits and nuts and chili, as well as others. Every time we change the product, the vats must be thoroughly cleaned, especially if we've been using chili.

The manufacturing machinery creates the different shapes of the product and you'll see whatever product is being manufactured at the time of your visit. Finally, the last part of the manufacturing process is the <u>wrapping</u> **(Q15)**. We use a foil and paper combination in two pieces, which is done on a horizontal flow wrapping machine. Foil is necessary to stop greasy cocoa butter getting from the inside of the package to the outside and the paper of course is branded on the outside to look attractive.

You now have some time to look at questions sixteen to twenty.

(20 second gap)

Now listen to the rest of the information talk and answer questions sixteen to twenty.

After the manufacturing process, you will return to the administration area. You will get to watch a film on the history of chocolate and then there will be a <u>short lecture</u> **(Q16)** that goes through the marketing and sales strategies of our firm. Of course, we don't give away any of our secrets!

At the end of the visit, you will of course get a tasting! All of our products will be available to taste and your <u>guide</u> **(Q17)** will assist you in choosing a selection. We recommend, especially with children, that you don't eat too much. As well as being too unhealthy, your bodies are not usually ready for so much rich food and it can upset your stomachs.

So, let me run through some administration for you. First of all, for individuals and small groups, we have one tour in the morning, starting at <u>ten</u> **(Q18)** a.m. and one in the afternoon, starting at two p.m. For these tours, adults pay <u>thirteen</u> **(Q19)** dollars, senior citizens pay nine dollars and children pay six dollars. Of course, we run larger groups and school tours as well. The usual fees apply, except for school tours. Children cost four dollars each and for every seven children there must be one member of the school staff. There's no charge for the staff. All our guides, by the way, have police screening for working with children. Larger tours can take place at any time during the day, though of course they must be booked in advance. We have free parking for cars and coaches and the whole factory is <u>wheelchair</u> **(Q20)** friendly. Guide dogs are welcome, except in the manufacturing areas for obvious reasons.

That is the end of part two. You will now have half a minute to check your answers.

(30 second gap)

Now turn to part three.

Part three. You will hear two students discussing a course change with their tutor. First you have some time to look at questions twenty-one to twenty-five.

(20 second gap)

Now listen carefully and answer questions twenty-one to twenty-five.

Edward   Professor Holden. Do you have a minute?

Professor Holden   Yes. Come in, both of you. What can I do for you?

Tina   We wanted to ask you about changing courses.

Professor Holden   Ah. Well, sit down for a while then. So, you two are studying history at the moment, is that right?

Edward   That's right.

Professor Holden   And why do you want to change?

Tina   Well, you know how in the first year, we had to study three different subjects, one of which was our main one?

Professor Holden   Yes. That's our way of making sure that you get a broader education. You can also have the chance to see if a different subject might suit you better.

Tina   That's what has happened to me. In my first year, I studied history, French and linguistics. Now it's the start of the second year, and I've found that it is the linguistics that I really miss. History is great, but I've found that there were too many <u>periods</u> **(Q21)** to study that I'm just not interested in.

Professor Holden   Have you talked to any of the History department about this? Have you found out all the syllabus for the next two years?

Tina   Yes. I've spoken to the head of department and got the whole schedule. I also spoke to the course secretary and some of the lecturers.

Page 181

Professor Holden   Do you know that in years two and three, you don't need to study everything? You can choose the periods that you find more interesting.

Tina   Yes, I know. The course secretary went through everything with me very carefully. The problem is that year three has most of the specialisation **(Q22)** and even then I'll have too many obligatory topics.

Professor Holden   What about you, Edward?

Edward   Well, I studied History, English and Earth Sciences. I chose Earth sciences, as I wanted one subject that would be really different to what I was used to. I was really good at sciences at school, so I didn't find it difficult at all.

Professor Holden   So, is that what you want to study now, or is it English?

Edward   I love the English and the History, but I can't handle all the essays **(Q23)** in both subjects.

Professor Holden   Yes, I understand that. But, are you sure that you will handle the change of choice from a main subject in the arts to one that is so different in the sciences?

Edward   I've thought about this all summer. I know it's a big switch, but I've done some extra reading **(Q24)** over the summer and I talked it over with my family.

Professor Holden   Have you spoken to any of the Earth Sciences department about it?

Edward   Oh yes. I spoke to a lot of the teachers and they asked me about my education background. They seemed to be satisfied that I could cope.

Professor Holden   I'm not so sure.

Edward   Well, I can't ever be totally sure, but it's what I really want to do. I know it'll be hard work. Earth sciences has more lectures, but the major assessments are smaller assignments and projects **(Q25)**. The exams are shorter, too.

You now have some time to look at questions twenty-six to thirty.

(20 second gap)

Now listen to the rest of the discussion and answer questions twenty-six to thirty.

Professor Holden   In order to change, there is a certain amount of paperwork. Both of you need first of all to fill in this form. You need to put the main subject you're studying and the subject that you want to study. You'll need some signatures on it, too.

Tina   Whose do we need, Professor Holden?

Professor Holden   You'll need your personal tutor's signature. For you, Tina, that's me of course, but I don't know for Edward. I'm not his tutor.

Edward   It's Doctor Flynn **(Q26-Q28)**.

Professor Holden   OK. Now, you'll need as well the signatures of the head of department of the subject to which you're transferring. For you, Edward, you want to switch to Earth Sciences, don't you?

Edward   That's right. Mr. Thomas is the head of Earth Sciences.

Professor Holden   That's true, but he's not the head of University Science, who is the person you'll need. That's Professor Atkins **(Q26-Q28)**. She's very busy, but if you give the form to Mr. Morton, her PA, he'll make sure the form gets signed and back to you quickly. For Tina, your new HOD will be Professor Coles.

Tina   OK.

Professor Holden   Finally, you'll both need the signature of the director. You'll need to get Miss Morgan's signature for that **(Q26-Q28)**. Doctor Tennant is on long-term sick leave and Miss Morgan is his short-term fill-in.

Edward   And do we need the signature from the department that we're leaving?

Professor Holden   The HOD for history is Professor Evans, but he'll hear about it through normal channels. He doesn't need to take part in this process.

Edward   OK. Thanks.

Professor Holden   Now, do you know what to do with these forms once you have all the signatures?

Tina   No. Can't we just give it to you?

Professor Holden   You can come and ask me any questions, but don't leave the finished form with me. You need to take the form to the registrar's office.

Edward   Can we email it?

Professor Holden   I know scanning and emailing is a lot easier, but the registrar's office will need the original.

Tina   What about post then?

Professor Holden   Posting is fine **(Q29)**. However, that might delay things. These kinds of changes can only be done quite near the start of the second year. If your paper gets lost in the post or stuck over a weekend, it might not work for you.

Tina   OK. How do we go there then?

Professor Holden   Go down to the railway station. Go past it and on the right will be the university administrative building. It faces the post office. Go to the second floor and ask if the registrar's office is open. It is often closed. If they tell you it's open, go up a floor to where it is and deliver your form **(Q30)**.

That is the end of part three. You will now have half a minute to check your answers.

(30 second gap)

Now turn to part four.

Part four. You will hear part of a geography lecture on Australia's Great Artesian Basin. First you have some time to look at questions thirty-one to forty.

(50 second gap)

Now listen carefully and answer questions thirty-one to forty.

Good morning ladies and gentleman and welcome to this geography lecture.

Occupying an area of over one point seven million square kilometres beneath the arid and semi-arid parts of Queensland, New South Wales, South Australia and the Northern Territory, the Great Artesian Basin covers almost a quarter of the Australian continent, and contains enough water to cover the world over. Much remains to be known about this valuable resource that has enabled life in inland Australia to develop over thousands of years.

To explain how the Great Artesian Basin works, you need to know how it came to exist in the first place. Back in the Triassic age, Australia was joined together with the other southern continents, including Antarctica, South America, Africa and New Zealand, in a land mass called Gondwana. Right up in the north west corner of Gondwana, there was a <u>natural dip **(Q31)**</u> that became the Great Artesian Basin. Over the next one hundred million years, huge events like ice ages in Europe and tectonic plate movements caused the ocean level to rise and fall. When the ocean levels rose, water became trapped in that natural dip and formed a sea. But when the ocean levels fell, the whole area became land again. When the seas drained away, they left <u>clay **(Q32)**</u> deposits behind, which hardened into impermeable stone strata.

These stone strata residues became the environment that allowed the formation of the Great Artesian Basin. Below ground level, where the ancient natural dip lies today, there is a layer of permeable stone allowing falling rain to seep through it. Where there is no impermeable stone, the water soaks down until it reaches <u>the saturation level **(Q33)**</u>, which is where the rock ends and the water reservoir of the Basin begins. The water in the reservoir is then held between two impermeable stone strata. This water is incredibly pure, as it has been filtered and cleaned as it passed from the permeable rock. The water then remains trapped under the ground, only emerging through <u>a natural spring **(Q34)**</u>.

Scientists estimate that there's over sixty-five thousand million megalitres of water in the Basin right now. A megalitre is a million litres. Sixty thousand million megalitres would be enough to cover all the land on the planet in almost half a metre of water. The water fortunately does not stay underground. For thousands and thousands of years, artesian water has been bubbling up to the surface all over the Basin area. This brings life to parts of Australia that would otherwise be barren desert. These areas are home to a host of native plant and animal species that have evolved in these unusual <u>ecosystems **(Q35)**</u>. Many of these can't be found anywhere else in the world. What's more, water from the Basin's springs around the recharge zones often seeps into natural creek and river systems, helping to keep them flowing when the rains don't come. Of course, not all the emerging water comes from natural escape. Farmers, town councils and others all create bore holes to make artesian wells and these have helped maintain agriculture and <u>urbanisation **(Q36)**</u> that wouldn't have been otherwise possible.

The trouble is that modern usage of the Basin's water has caused the Great Artesian Basin problems. It's so bad that a lot of bores and natural springs have simply stopped flowing, and hundreds of bores that do flow are out of control. They can't be turned off, and they're wasting millions of litres of water every day. A lot of bore water flows into shallow channels dug into the dirt, which encourage noxious weeds and feral animals, and it's almost pointless, because the open channels or drains mean around ninety-five per cent of the water evaporates **(Q37)** or seeps away before it can even be used. Meanwhile, to make matters worse, a lot of old bores were poorly made, or the casings underground are corroding, so the water is escaping to the wrong places and damaging the environment.

There are, however, things we can do. These days, there's a strategy in place to fix up the old bores so they can be used in a sustainable way, and the water can be distributed more responsibly. This process involves what we call capping and piping. Put simply, capping is just like putting a lid on the bores. Through a tap system **(Q38)**, farmers can turn the bores on and off and only use the water when it's needed. Piping involves replacing the old open channels or drains with new piping. Although this is a lengthy and expensive process, it is regarded as one of the best ways to preserve a lot of the water that is needlessly lost. Government funding has allowed the process of piping to be carried out for a number of years now and, because of this, the water goes straight to tanks **(Q39)** without being wasted, and it doesn't ruin the native landscape by encouraging weeds and feral animals.

This effort to make the water usage is vital. The Great Artesian Basin is key to life to about a quarter of the country, but it also impacts Australians from coast to coast. In fact, it impacts the country so much that if it was to dry up, Australia would be a very different place. Seventy towns that still rely on the Basin for their water would disappear. The beef, wool and sheep industries would lose about one billion Australian dollars a year, and the food production system would be affected very badly. Australia would have to import more food and the balance of payments **(Q40)** would change affecting the country's economy as a whole.

That is the end of part four. You will now have half a minute to check your answers.

(30 second gap)

That is the end of listening test four.

LISTENING TEST 5 TRANSCRIPT

This recording is copyright by Robert Nicholson and Simone Braverman, all rights reserved.

IELTS listening practice tests. Test five. In the IELTS test you hear some recordings and you have to answer questions on them. You have time to read the instructions and questions and check your work. All recordings are played only once. The test is in four parts. Now turn to part one.

Part one. You will hear a conversation between a man and a woman discussing a train ticket.

First you have some time to look at questions one to five.

(20 second gap)

Now we begin. You should answer the questions as you listen, as the recording is not played twice. Listen carefully to the conversation and answer questions one to five.

Roger	Good morning. Welcome to Southern Trains. What can I do for you today?
Sandra	Good morning. Can I get train tickets here?
Roger	Yes, you can.
Sandra	Good. I'd like to buy a season ticket, please.
Roger	That's no problem. First of all, I'd like to take some personal information.
Sandra	OK.
Roger	So, what is your full name?
Sandra	I'm Sandra Williams. That's S - A - N - D - R - A and then W - I - L - L - I - A - M - S **(Q1)**.
Roger	Thank you. And can I have your full address, including the postal code?
Sandra ED.	It's forty-three **(Q2)** Andover Way. The town is Stanton and the postal code is ST six, three
Roger	Thank you. Now I need your date of birth.
Sandra	It's the eighth of October, nineteen ninety-four **(Q3)**.
Roger	Have you had a season ticket with us before?
Sandra	No, this is the first time.
Roger	That's fine. Now, your season ticket can be registered online. To set up an account, we send you an email with details of what to do. So, can I have your email address, please?
Sandra	I'm not that keen on giving out my email address. I get too much spam.

Roger   I can understand that. I can assure you that we don't send you any other emails at all and the address is kept confidential. We are bound to that by law.

Sandra   I suppose that's OK. My address is sandra at primrose dot com. Primrose is spelled <u>P - R - I - M - R - O - S - E</u> **(Q4)**.

Roger   And finally, I need a contact number for you.

Sandra   Is it OK if I just give you my cell number?

Roger   Yes, that's fine.

Sandra   It's oh five <u>four eight two</u> **(Q5)**, four nine five, seven one two.

Roger   Thank you. That is all the personal information done then.

Before the conversation continues, you have some time to look at questions six to ten.

(20 second gap)

Now listen carefully and answer questions six to ten.

Roger   Now I need some details about the season ticket. What journey do you need it for?

Sandra   <u>I've just got a new job in Bexington and I've quit my old job in Petersfield. I was thinking of driving to the new job, but there's always too much traffic when you pass Amberton. I thought the train would therefore be better for the commute trip from here in Stanton</u> **(Q6)**.

Roger   I think you're right to do that. Trains don't get held up by traffic jams! Do you want just that route? For a little more, I can get you a ticket for the whole region.

Sandra   I'm not sure yet. I'll see when you give me the actual prices.

Roger   Of course. Now the price also depends on the timings. Off-peak is much cheaper of course. That's for leaving after nine thirty in the morning and for not returning between the hours of four and six in the afternoon.

Sandra   Saving money would be good, but <u>I'll need a peak ticket. I'll need to keep normal work hours and also not be too late back home to look after the children when they get back from school.</u>

Roger   <u>Another way to save would be to buy only a weekday season ticket and not travel on weekends. Would that be good for you?</u>

Sandra   <u>Let's think. I do have some family near my new job, but I don't think I'd travel too often by train at weekends there. I'd probably drive with the family. The weekday thing would be an excellent option for me</u> **(Q7)**.

Roger   OK. I'll make it that. Finally, would you like first class, second class or variable class?

Page 187

Sandra	What's the variable class?

Roger   That is something for frequent travellers. Travellers get twelve individual journeys a calendar month in first class and the rest of the month in second class. That way, you can treat yourself from time to time when you're tired or get some peace and quiet when the train is busy.

Sandra   I think I'll go for that **(Q8)**. I hate it when there are too many noisy kids on a train.

Roger   So, now for the prices. For a one-month ticket for your route it is one hundred and ninety-eight dollars. If you go for the whole region, it will be two hundred and fifteen dollars. If you want a ticket for more than one month, it's the same price per month, until you go for a ticket for six months or longer. Then there is a twenty per cent discount, which would make it one hundred and fifty-eight dollars and forty cents per month for your route, or one hundred and seventy-two dollars for the whole region.

Sandra   I think I'll just go for my route rather than the whole region, but I'll take a six month ticket and get the discount **(Q9)**.

Roger   That's fine. It'll be one hundred and fifty-eight forty then. I've just put in all the information. Please wait for a couple of minutes for the computer to process the order. The ticket will then be printed out.

Sandra   Where would I go to catch my train here every morning? Is it still platform four?

Roger   It used to be that one, but it's changed now to seven **(Q10)**. When you come in through the entrance, there are six platforms right in front of you. That's where platform four is. To get to yours, go right as you come in and you'll find it just beyond the wall on the right side of the station.

Sandra   OK.

That is the end of part one. You will now have half a minute to check your answers.

(30 second gap)

Now turn to part two.

Part two. You will hear a woman giving some people information about some hotel services. First you have some time to look at questions eleven to fifteen.

(20 second gap)

Now listen carefully to the information talk and answer questions eleven to fifteen.

Hello, everyone. My name is Anna. I'd like to welcome you all today to the Paradise Hotel and I'll tell you now a little about the services we have on offer here.

As you've probably noticed, the Paradise Hotel is built on a hill and so its design reflects that. Our hotel is on seven levels and I'd quickly like to explain what can be found on each level. The main entrance to the hotel and <u>the reception is on level three. You can find the concierge's desk there **(Q11)** </u>and also our coffee bar with its great view over the hotel's swimming pools, beach and sea. <u>All our accommodation is on levels four, five and six. If your room is on level four, then its number will start with a four, for example four oh seven **(Q12)**</u>, and if your room is on level five, then its number will start with a five, for example five two three. The same goes for level six. Level seven gives access to the spa and treatment area. If you'd like to book a treatment there or just use some of facilities, call it from the phone in your room or just go down and speak to the staff there. <u>Level seven also gives access to the swimming pools and, beyond them, the beach **(Q13)**.</u> Both the beach and the swimming pools have sun loungers, where you can lie and enjoy the good weather. There are also snack kiosks and bars found around the pools and beach.

Moving up from the reception level, <u>level two is where all the hotel restaurants are. There are three to choose from. First, there is the Chef's restaurant, where you can eat breakfast, lunch and dinner from the buffets provided. If you'd prefer to eat á la carte, the Eastern restaurant does Asian specialities, such as Thai, Indian and Chinese food, and the Ocean restaurant specialises in seafood and fish **(Q14)**</u>. Again, places can be booked for the Eastern and Ocean restaurants from your room phone or you can book at reception on level three or just go to the restaurant itself.

<u>Level one has our Fitness Area. This includes a fully equipped gym with weights and aerobic machinery and class rooms, where you can go for scheduled fitness classes, such as aerobics, pilates, yoga or spinning **(Q15)**.</u> The schedules are all posted at the Fitness Area's reception and at the main hotel reception.

You now have some time to look at questions sixteen to twenty.

(20 second gap)

Now listen to the rest of the information talk and answer questions sixteen to twenty.

Now I'd like to let you know about some of the things that are going on this week at the hotel.

Today's Monday and tonight we have an entertainment evening by the pool. The weather forecast is good and you should enjoy our selection of dancers, singers, magician and other acts. This will start at seven and go on until <u>ten **(Q16)**</u>.

Tomorrow, <u>we have a pub style quiz, which will be held in the rooftop bar **(Q17)**.</u> You can access this if you go up to the gym and follow the stairs opposite where the lift opens. The quiz will start at eight in the evening and go on for around two hours. Please note that under eighteens will not be allowed in the bar.

On Wednesday, we have a karaoke night. This will start at seven and go on until nine. This will take place next to the pool and you are invited to be brave, grab the microphone and show everyone what you can do. <u>To start the evening, the hotel manager has bravely volunteered to sing first with his favourite song **(Q18)**.</u> He hasn't told us what his song is yet!

We have left Thursday evening free. Some people just like to be left alone to relax and there is a travelling circus visiting the town and this is only one kilometre away. Let us know if you'd like us to book you a taxi to and back from the circus if you'd like to go.

Page 189

Friday evening is our jazz night. We have a local jazz band who plays with us every week and they are a firm favourite with all our guests. This takes place in the coffee bar lounge and in order to see them, you need to book a table. We only have forty tables available with five places at each, so make sure you book ahead, so that you won't be disappointed. Booking a table costs thirty dollars and <u>bookings should be done at the reception</u> **(Q19)**, not the coffee bar.

Saturday and Sunday are also left free, though there will be <u>some live music playing both evenings by the pool</u> **(Q20)**, from seven until half past nine.

Now, I have posted this schedule of events on the entertainments noticeboard and it's also available on our hotel website. If you'd like to ask me any questions about anything, please do so at any time. I'm usually in my office, which is next to reception. If I'm not there, ask reception, and they'll page me.

That is the end of part two. You will now have half a minute to check your answers.

(30 second gap)

Now turn to part three.

Part three. You will hear four students discussing their geography project. First you have some time to look at questions twenty-one to twenty-five.

(20 second gap)

Now listen carefully and answer questions twenty-one to twenty-five.

Tony   Hi Alison. How are you?

Alison   Hi Tony. I'm good. Are the other two here yet?

Tony   Not yet. Oh, here they are now. Hi Greg. Hi Sophie.

Greg   Hi Tony. Hi Alison.

Sophie   Hi guys! Are we late?

Tony   Not at all. Well, let's get down to it right away. As you know, we're talking about our geography project today and our task is to survey an area to see whether it would be suitable for a new supermarket. Alison, you told me yesterday that you had an idea of how to start.

Alison   Yes. Well, the first thing is that we'll have to choose the actual site that we wish to survey. Once that's done, we'll need to do certain preparation work.

Greg   So, does anyone have any idea of a suitable site to survey? Sophie. You're good at this.

Sophie   Thanks, Greg. I've got some ideas. There is a farmer's field on Castle Road, just after the road leaves town and goes over the bridge. That could be a good place. Another possible site I found was in the town centre at the old cigarette factory. Finally, there's a possible site at the airport. Here are some notes I made for everyone. How's that, Greg?

Greg   Excellent. I like the one at the cigarette factory. That'll be great for people to go to without having to travel too far. I also think that the town council **(Q21)** would provide grants to help develop that site, as it's been abandoned for a long time.

Alison   That's true, Greg, but if you look at Sophie's notes, it says that the size of the site is limited. Not that many people will go on foot and, while there'll be enough room for the actual supermarket building, there'll be no room for a car park **(Q22)**.

Tony   That's a good point, Alison. The potential cost of the site will be a lot higher too, as it's in the town centre.

Greg   It's just a project, though. We won't actually need to buy a site.

Tony   No, but doing costs in the project will all be part of how we're assessed. We will need to look at all start-up costs, as well as income forecasts **(Q23)** for the first ten years of operation.

Greg   OK. I see that it's important.

Alison   I like the idea of the site by the river. It shouldn't be too expensive and the site near the edge of the town would be good for people to get to. There's the town's ring road that goes nearby the site as well.

Tony   Yes. However, the problem I see with that site is that it's too close to the river. We've had years with lots of rain recently and the river's been known to burst its banks. There would maybe have to be a great deal of protection building **(Q24)** to be done.

Alison   I suppose that would be something that our survey would address.

Sophie   In fact, that might be something extra for us to explore that we wouldn't normally have the opportunity to study. It could work in our favour.

Greg   And now the airport site?

Tony   It seems there's nothing particularly challenging about that site. The land wouldn't be too expensive and there's plenty of road access **(Q25)** because of the people going to the airport.

Sophie   Actually, I heard airport sites can be quite expensive.

Greg   Yes. And although there is plenty of road access, the airport is not actually that close to the town. It's not that convenient.

You now have some time to look at questions twenty-six to thirty.

(20 second gap)

Now listen to the rest of the discussion and answer questions twenty-six to thirty.

Tony   So, I think we all agree on the Castle Road site next to the river. So, Sophie. What's next?

Sophie   We really need to decide who does what. There are a number of jobs to be done before we actually get to go to the field and survey it. If we can get everything done quickly, we can do the survey at the weekend.

Greg   So, what's the first thing?

Sophie   We need to get authorisation from the farmer to be on his land. If we can't do that, there's no point in starting to gather any information **(Q26)**.

Alison   I can do that. I'll nip down to the town surveyor's office and find the name and address of the owner. I'll go straight away and talk to him or her.

Sophie   Thanks, Alison. Now, one of the important early things is to find out whether there are any other development plans scheduled for that specific area or in any other area that would affect what we're planning.

Greg   I can try and do that, but I'm not sure what the procedure is **(Q27)**.

Tony   It's easy, Greg. You just go down to the surveyor's office again and ask for all proposed plans for that postcode. I can text you the postcode later.

Greg   Thanks, Tony **(Q28)**. That's my job organised then.

Sophie   Now, when we start to survey the field, we'll need certain equipment. You asked about equipment, didn't you, Alison?

Alison   I spoke to Professor Johnson yesterday and we can borrow all the necessary equipment from the department. I'll check that all the equipment is free at the weekend **(Q29)**.

Greg   Good. Anything else?

Alison   Yes, Professor Johnson also told me that we have to pay a two hundred pound deposit for the equipment.

Greg   I don't have that kind of money.

Tony   I can pay the deposit as long as I get it back. My parents have just put some money in the bank from a job I did for the summer **(Q30)**. I can get it from the bank when we need it.

Alison   It should only be for two days, Tony. We can get everything done in that time.

Tony   OK. I'll pay the deposit and pick up the equipment from the department.

Alison   Don't get it just yet. We have to get the authorisation to be on the land first.

Tony   OK.

Sophie   So, if we can get all these jobs done over the next three days, we can meet again on Thursday. If all is OK, we could get the equipment on Friday and survey the field at the weekend.

Alison	Good.
Greg	Well, thanks everyone. I'd better be off. Bye.
Sophie	Bye.
Alison	Bye.

That is the end of part three. You will now have half a minute to check your answers.

(30 second gap)

Now turn to part four.

Part four. You will hear part of a lecture on tea. First you have some time to look at questions thirty-one to forty.

(50 second gap)

Now listen carefully and answer questions thirty-one to forty.

Today's lecture is about a product that has become a social custom in many countries: tea.

Tea is first recorded as being drunk in China **(Q31)**, with the first records of it dating from around two hundred years BC. In fact, tea drinking certainly became established in China many centuries before it had even been heard of in the west. In the latter half of the sixteenth century, there are the first mentions of tea as a drink among Europeans. These are mostly from Portuguese, who were living in the East as traders and missionaries. Although some of these individuals may have brought back samples of tea to their native country, it was not the Portuguese who were the first to ship back tea as a commercial import. This was done by the Dutch, who in the last years of the sixteenth century began to encroach on Portuguese trading routes **(Q32)** in the East.

In the seventeenth century, the British took to tea with an enthusiasm that continues to the present day. It became a popular drink in coffee houses, which were as much locations for the transaction of business, as they were for relaxation or pleasure. Coffee houses were thought to be the preserve of middle- and upper-class men, as women drank tea in their own homes, and then tea was still too expensive to be widespread among the working classes. In part, its high price was due to a punitive system of tax. The first tax **(Q33)** on tea in the leaf, introduced in Britain in 1689, was so high at twenty-five pence per pound that it almost stopped sales. It was gradually reduced until as recently as 1964, when tea tax was finally abolished. British politicians were forever tinkering with the exact rate and method.

During the eighteenth century, there was an equally furious argument about whether tea drinking was good or bad for the health. Wealthy philanthropists in particular worried that excessive tea drinking among the working classes would lead to weakness and melancholy. Typically, they were not concerned with the continuing popularity of tea among the wealthy classes, for whom strength for labour was of rather less importance! The debate rumbled on into the nineteenth century, but was really put to an end in the middle of that century, when a new generation of wealthy philanthropists realised the value of tea drinking to the temperance movement. In their enthusiasm to have the working classes go teetotal, tea was regularly offered at temperance meetings as a substitute for alcohol **(Q34)**.

Today, tea is a staggeringly popular drink all over the world. Although many people perceive the UK to be the biggest tea consumer, they only make up six per cent **(Q35)** of world tea consumption, which is the same as Russia **(Q36)**. Japan, another traditional tea consumer, makes up five per cent. Chinese consumption outstrips these countries with sixteen per cent, but India **(Q37)** is the largest consumer with twenty-three per cent. The rest of the tea consumption across the world is shared around the rest of the world.

Producing tea is a careful process. For optimum taste, the best quality teas are grown at tea gardens at an altitude of five thousand to seven thousand feet above sea level. It begins with plucking, the removal of the right parts from the tea plant, Camellia sinensis. Pluckers are specially trained to only select two leaves and a bud. Plucking is maintained at about seven day intervals. The plucked leaves are collected in baskets, taking care that the leaves are not crushed by overloading. The leaves and buds then need to be withered. During the withering process, the leaf is induced to lose moisture **(Q38)** to prepare it for further processing. Normally this is carried out by spreading tea leaves thinly on troughs through which warm air is circulated by fans. The average length of the withering time depends greatly on the quality of the leaf peculiar to the region where it has been grown.

When satisfactory withering has taken place, the leaf is ready for rolling. This process uses grooved rollers that twist the leaves, break them up and take out the juices. Leaves pass through three to four such rollers, getting reduced in size and their cells **(Q39)** broken up to enable fermentation. Normally the tea ferments or oxidises from sixty to a hundred minutes, depending upon the leaf quality. The character of the tea develops significantly during the fermentation process. The next part of the process is drying. The objective of drying is to arrest fermentation and remove any dampness from the tea. After completion of the drying process, the tea becomes fully black in colour.

The teas are then sorted, graded and packed. The tea is sold at auctions **(Q40)** to traders who then employ tasters to decide how the teas should be blended to create the specific brands or retail requirements.

That is the end of part four. You will now have half a minute to check your answers.

(30 second gap)

That is the end of listening test five.

Made in the USA
Las Vegas, NV
07 August 2023

75789868R00109